"Once again Robbie Steinhouse helps us push boundaries by bringing more artistry to the two fields of NLP and coaching by integrating NLP technology with the task and relationship of coaching."

Judith DeLozier, NLP Founding Member

"In this well-crafted book, Robbie Steinhouse offers a beautiful integration of NLP into the still emerging field of coaching. His frameworks are exceptionally clear, the examples are lucid and helpful, and the range of techniques is impressive. I strongly recommend the book for all those interested in helping others on the path to creative change!"

Stephen Gilligan, Ph.D., author of *The Courage to Love* **and** *The Hero's Journey*

"A captivating and insightful book that brings coaching and NLP together. Robbie's personal insights, the processes he describes and the fascinating historical asides make this a valuable reference to keep nearby."

Shelle Rose Charvet, author of *The Customer is Bothering Me* **and** *Words that Change Minds*

"Robbie Steinhouse is an accomplished author, businessman, musician and, I believe, one of the best NLP coaches in the UK today. His style is fluid, easy to read and understand. This book will not only change your beliefs, but may change your life; a highly recommended bible of NLP techniques and values."

Jimmy D Contractor, Company Secretary, Tata Limited

G000291644

"This accessible book provides a rigorous and thorough framework for using NLP in a professional coaching context. Whether you are just starting out on your coaching journey or you are a seasoned veteran, this book is an important reference for your library."

Kimberley Hare, Kaizen Training Limited

"An excellent guide for those who know coaching but not NLP, those who know NLP but not coaching, for those at the start of their professional coaching career, and for every coach who knows we learn something new every day (which I hope means every coach!)."

Julie Hay, Teacher and Supervisor (Transactional Analyst), author of *Reflective Practice* and *Supervision for Coaches*

"I always say that the more successful you are, the more you need coaching! *How to Coach with NLP* shows, from both the coaching and client perspective, how to design the life you want to lead and the business you want to create. I thoroughly recommend it."

Mike Southon, *Financial Times* columnist and best-selling business author

"How to Coach with NLP is a great practical guide to using the tools and techniques of NLP in a work or coaching environment. Robbie has a great common sense, jargon-free approach which means this book is really accessible and practical."

Matt Foster, Assistant Editor, BBC York

"There is something of value in this book for everyone; it's an essential tool for Coaches, NLP Practitioners and anyone seeking to resolve issues and understand better how the mind works."

Tony Felix, Personal Trainer, Martial Arts Champion and Coach, Tai Chi Champion and Teacher, NLP Master Practitioner

"Robbie's voice is entirely his own and he has a very entertaining way of making the techniques of NLP (and other disciplines) easily accessible to all. You can put the exercises in this book to immediate and practical use."

Hilary Cochrane, ICF Master Certified Coach

"As a professional coach who sees NLP as a central pillar to effective coaching, I was delighted when I heard Robbie was writing this book. It's a must-read for anyone looking for a practical understanding of the inner and outer game of getting results."

Donald MacNaughton, Olympic & Football Premier League Coach

How to Coach with NLP

Robbie Steinhouse

**Prentice Hall
Business
is an imprint of**

Harlow, England • London • New York • Boston • San Francisco • Toronto • Sydney • Singapore • Hong Kong
Tokyo • Seoul • Taipei • New Delhi • Cape Town • Madrid • Mexico City • Amsterdam • Munich • Paris • Milan

PEARSON EDUCATION LIMITED

Edinburgh Gate
Harlow CM20 2JE
Tel: +44 (0)1279 623623
Fax: +44 (0)1279 431059
Website: www.pearsoned.co.uk

First published in Great Britain in 2010

© Robbie Steinhouse 2010

The right of Robbie Steinhouse to be identified as author of this work has been asserted by
him in accordance with the Copyright, Designs and Patents Act 1988.

Pearson Education is not responsible for the content of third party internet sites.

ISBN: 978-0-273-73839-8

British Library Cataloguing-in-Publication Data
A catalogue record for this book is available from the British Library

Library of Congress Cataloging-in-Publication Data
Steinhouse, Robbie.
  How to coach with NLP / Robbie Steinhouse.
    p. cm.
  Includes bibliographical references and index.
  ISBN 978-0-273-73839-8 (pbk. : alk. paper) 1. Neurolinguistic programming. 2.
Personal coaching. I. Title.
  BF637.N46S74 2010
  158'.9--dc22

                                                                  2010030680

10 9 8 7 6 5 4 3 2 1
14 13 12 11 10

Typeset in 10pt IowanOldStyle by 3
Printed in Great Britain by Henry Ling Ltd., at the Dorset Press, Dorchester, Dorset

Contents

About the author

Robbie Steinhouse has many years' experience of both NLP and coaching. He is a certified NLP trainer and head of training at NLP School in London. He is an ICF certified coach and managing director of the Coaching Consultancy, and has worked in a wide range of coaching contexts. As an executive coach and NLP trainer he has worked with numerous clients in business, government and the third sector, including Accenture, the Bank of England, the BBC, Coca Cola, Disney Corp, HSBC, KPMG, the NHS, Rolls Royce, Tesco, Vodafone, the UN and the Red Cross.

Robbie is also a successful entrepreneur and the author of *Think Like an Entrepreneur* (2008) and *Brilliant Decision Making* (2010).

Author's acknowledgements

The book is dedicated to Robert Dilts. Robert was one of the original group of students at the University of California at Santa Cruz when NLP was created in the 1970s: since that time he has professionalised and systematised the discipline and in my view has become its leading thinker. He is the creator of a number of the NLP coaching models and processes in this book. He is also one of the best coaches in the world; it was at the 2003 International Coaching Federation annual conference, where he was the keynote speaker, that I got to know him and received an informal coaching session that changed my life. During that session, I was amazed by the complexity and naturalness of Robert's coaching. He used a mixture of techniques, examples and humanity in such an elegant and affirming way that I had to find out what he was doing and how he did it! I hope this book goes some way to answering those questions.

I would like to thank my long-term writing coach and editor, Chris West, who has again helped me enormously in compiling this book. As a student at NLP School and as a recipient of a few coaching sessions, he retains a thoughtful scepticism and will not buy into NLP orthodoxy unless it actually makes sense. He is a brilliant foil and has really helped me shape this book. If you want to write any kind of book, be it a novel, a business book or a self-help classic – he can be found at chris@chriswest.info.

I also want to thank my commissioning editor, Samantha Jackson, at Pearson Education for commissioning this work. She studied NLP with me in her spare time and provided the vision and structure for this book. Along with her gift for writing, no-nonsense approach and clarity of thought, she has really helped shape this project and bring it to fruition.

Thanks too to Hilary Cochrane, my coaching supervisor, who was my expert adviser on this project and helped me develop the contracting material in this book, and to my long-time friend and coach Ann Baldwin: the best way to learn to coach is to receive coaching from the best. This also applies to my other coaches, Tony Felix and Lois Evans, who have helped me in so many positive ways.

I have been lucky enough to both study and work with the best in NLP and coaching, and would like to thank them for all I have learnt from them. Thank you Robert Dilts (again!), Judith Delozier, Stephen Gilligan, Shelle Rose Charvet, Ian McDermott, Jan Elfin, Deborah Bacon Dilts, Suzi Smith, Richard Bandler, John Grinder, Stephen Covey, Kimberley Hare, Anthony Robbins, Joseph O'Connor, Katie Hogg, Alison Underwood, Tad James, Aina Egeberg, Edward Hines, Sheena Reid, Antoine Bebe, Donald MacNaughton and Charles Faulkner.

Lastly, a big thank you to the many NLP students and coaching clients I have worked with over the years. It has been an honour to be part of their journey and has provided me with the experience I needed to write this book.

All authors like to hear from readers: if you find this book helpful but want to ask further questions (or just comment), do get in touch. My email is robbie@nlpschool.com. I look forward to hearing from you.

Preface

It is both a great honour and a great pleasure to write this preface to Robbie Steinhouse's new book *How to Coach with NLP*. As one of the original developers of NLP, I am impressed with the way that Robbie has been able to capture the essence of the discipline with such clarity and simplicity. It is especially rewarding for me to see how Robbie has integrated my own ideas – such as the NeuroLogical Levels, the Hero's Journey, the Meta Mirror and the creativity process modelled on Walt Disney – into the coaching framework. In addition, Robbie has added his own special insights to make these processes highly accessible to professional coaches.

Ever since its origins in the 1970s, the vision of NLP has been to provide simple, life-transforming tools for everyone, to help them attain personal goals, resolve family and relationship issues, enhance learning and creativity, increase physical and mental health, strengthen their capacity for leadership and team cooperation, and succeed in business. In *How to Coach with NLP*, Robbie has taken NLP another important step towards realising that vision.

How to Coach with NLP is well-structured, well-written and provides an excellent overview of how the fundamentals of contemporary NLP can be effectively applied through coaching and integrated with other coaching methodologies. Robbie's writing style is lucid, direct and practical. It is one of the teachings of NLP that 'knowledge is only a rumour until it is in the muscle'; Robbie provides exercises and real-life examples that create a solid bridge between knowing and doing.

I have known Robbie for over seven years now. He is a deeply devoted student of NLP and a skilled coach and trainer, receiving his NLP Trainer certification through NLP University in Santa Cruz, California. His understanding of NLP is enhanced by the fact that he has applied it to his own life and truly 'walks the talk'.

How to Coach with NLP is an important resource both for practitioners of NLP who want to become better coaches and for coaches who want to make their sessions more effective by using NLP. It is also a marvellous introduction to NLP and coaching for anyone looking for tools to bring out the best in themselves and to help others to do the same.

Robert B. Dilts
NLP founding member, world renowned trainer, writer and coach
Santa Cruz, California
July 2010

How to use this book

I have written this book with three audiences in mind:

- Coaches or people who use coaching as part of their job
- People already trained in NLP
- People interested in using coaching or NLP in their personal and professional lives.

For coaches, the NLP approaches to building rapport and trust in Part I provide specific steps to follow that can overcome any tension felt in a session. Also in Part I, the NLP methods for understanding the inner world of the client provide a very practical form of applied psychology, which you can begin to use immediately, picking up linguistic and physical cues and putting them to use at once for the client's benefit. The NLP coaching processes in Part II provide a toolkit to help clients towards goals, creativity and life purpose. There are also techniques to tackle deep issues, from nerves and problematic relationships to limiting beliefs and low self-esteem. To make these processes as practical as possible, I have included coach scripts and many transcripts of live coaching sessions. Lastly, in Part III, I cover a range of different types of coaching from organisational to 'life': if you focus mainly on one area of coaching, I hope you find there will be some useful cross-over material from both my organisational experience and my work as a life coach.

For people trained in NLP, the contracting section in Part I provides the key to using NLP in a professional context. I have also included a full transcript, in Appendix C, of a contracting session to make this as explicit as possible. Often those trained in NLP are not aware of the professional process required to set out the 'ground rules' for this type of relationship; this is hugely important as it honours one of the key tenets of NLP, 'pacing and leading'. If the ground rules are set well, the client is paced into the subsequent processes and ideas; if this is not done well, the client may not really engage with NLP and may actually resent its use. The NLP saying 'an ounce of framing is better than a pound of reframing' equally refers to the application of NLP itself. Also, coaching brings with it a more 'client-led' approach which I incorporate in my use of NLP generally.

Many of the processes in Part II are based on ones that will be familiar to people trained in NLP (though as there are so many processes in NLP, I hope some will be new to such readers). Even if you know most of the processes, you will find that I have amended them in places: over many years of coaching and training I have found certain small changes make a big difference. There are also two original processes, Rescripting and Permission, that I developed myself.

Although this book is about coaching in a professional context, I have made every effort to make it relevant for people who want to use an NLP coaching approach as a manager, as a parent, as an adviser, as a friend – or, most importantly, as a tool for their own personal development.

I shall explain the main NLP terms as I go through the book, in the text and via an 'NLP Dictionary'. For a wider and deeper glossary of NLP terms and concepts, please visit www. nlpschool.com.

Introduction: coaching and NLP – a perfect match?

"A good head and a good heart are always a formidable combination."

Nelson Mandela

In this section, I shall discuss the two disciplines of coaching and NLP and how they complement each other. Then I shall present a specific NLP coaching model that I shall be referring to throughout the book.

Coaching and NLP share a fundamental purpose: to help people live happier and more fulfilling lives. However, they are rarely taught together, which I find strange.

I believe that NLP is the secret that makes coaching so powerful. It takes the mystique of the great coach and breaks it down so it can be learnt by anyone, taking the implicit approach of coaching and making it explicit and understandable. In support of this belief, I find that most of the best coaches I come across have also studied NLP.

The two disciplines are effectively made for each other. In this book I shall show both why this is the case and how, on a practical level, they can be melded together to create something more powerful than either on its own.

I shall begin with very brief histories of the two disciplines, for readers unfamiliar with them.

A very brief history of coaching ...

In the 1970s in California a tennis coach who had been influenced by the 1960s' generation tried a new permissive approach to his job: he basically let the students have a go and didn't interfere with too much 'teaching'. The results were so powerful that a TV documentary was made about him – it tried to mock his methods, by getting him to teach an overweight woman with no tennis experience. But she learnt very fast. The coach, Tim Gallwey, wrote *The Inner Game of Tennis* and a number of other books in the 'Inner Game' series. The principle was transferred into business by a British student of his, John Whitmore, who wrote *Coaching for Performance*.

Meanwhile, new trends in both therapy and business were evolving.

In the 1960s a therapist called Carl Rogers began to challenge the medical approach of Freud and developed what he call 'client-centred therapy'. The principle behind this approach was to treat the client as an equal and hold him or her in what Rogers called 'unconditional positive regard'.

In the 1950s and 1960s, as the field of business became professionalised, and business schools and MBA programmes began to spread across the world, organisational models began to mushroom. Peter Drucker, a professor at NYU, became the founder of a new profession: the business philosopher.

These new approaches to sports, therapy and business – the inner game for sports, the Rogerian therapeutic relationship, and a more structured approach to career success – combined to create a new field called 'coaching'. There are now over 120,000 coaches working across the world and a number of coach-accreditation bodies, the largest of which is the International Coaching Federation. Coaching both formally and informally is a feature of many of the world's largest organisations, including HSBC, GSK and the BBC.

Life coaching has also become a huge growth area. It is a central tenet of this that the coach 'coaches the client's entire life': coaching is no longer simply a business tool but a holistic means of personal development in personal and even spiritual life.

... and of NLP

NLP stands for neuro-linguistic programming. NLP studies the mind, and how it programmes itself (and can be re-programmed) using languages (verbal language, but also the languages of physical sensations, gestures, etc.).

At the University of California in Santa Cruz in 1972, Richard Bandler, a mathematics student, and John Grinder, a linguistics professor, informally studied the work of Fritz Perls, the founder of Gestalt therapy, and family therapist Virginia Satir. The two therapists claimed to follow very different methods and yet they actually seemed to do exactly the same thing within the client sessions themselves – challenging limiting beliefs of their clients with very similar questions. Bandler and Grinder analysed the language patterns of these questions and produced a model (which will be outlined in Chapter 5) enabling non-therapists to use these questions.

NLP has blossomed since then, with a range of people adding insights and techniques, most of these for personal development, though NLP has also very successfully transitioned into the business world. This blossoming has been without the guidance of a unifying professional body – the founders could not agree on what form such a body would take. NLP has grown organically into a global psychological discipline without any clear boundaries. The benefit of this approach has been an enormous flow of creativity; the disadvantage is a lack of a commonly agreed approach to a teaching syllabus, standard practice and accreditation.

The presuppositions of NLP

One feature common to most schools of NLP is that they share a set of 'presuppositions', beliefs about people and change. The ones that follow are those most relevant to coaching and provide an excellent starting point for looking at the two disciplines in depth and seeing what they can add to each other.

- **People have all the resources they need** – Many NLP techniques are about transferring 'resources' (= useful things; more specifically, in coaching, useful states of mind) from one context to another. For example, if someone is fearful of selling but is very comfortable and charming in a social situation, they have the resources (charm and ease) necessary for selling; they just need to be able to mobilise them in the sales situation. NLP will help them do this.

- **There is no such thing as failure, only feedback** – NLP was influenced by early computer programs that taught themselves games like chess, which learnt – very effectively – this way. This attitude towards learning and change is ideal for human beings too. It is much, much better than the alternative, where something going wrong can lead to someone labelling themselves as 'a failure'.

- **All behaviour has a positive intention** – Self-defeating behaviour may seem to have no 'positive intention' at all. However, separating the behaviour from its root cause can have profoundly useful implications. NLP believes that human behaviour always starts from a positive place; although the behaviour may be self-defeating now, the intention behind it once had a positive purpose, and unless that original positive purpose can be met in an alternative way, the person will not be able to stop the self-defeating behaviour. A simple example is shouting at people, which is negative behaviour; however, if that person used to shout as a child and found it an effective way of asserting boundaries, then unless that person can find a new way to assert boundaries, the shouting behaviour will continue. This presupposition will appear in various guises throughout the book and is specifically covered in Chapter 10.

■ **A map is not the territory** – This presupposition may sound obvious, but there is an important truth behind it. People often have very fixed views of what is 'reality', but actually they mean *their interpretation* of reality. These views can clash, sometimes with disastrous consequences: numerous wars between different religious groups are examples. NLP is curious about how people form these maps, about how we can develop our own maps to make them more flexible, about how we can communicate with people who have different maps, and about how we can help people who seem to be victims of their own inflexible maps.

■ **In any interaction, the person with the greatest flexibility has most influence on the outcome** – NLP values flexibility highly – as does coaching. A good coach is a flexible coach, one who is not bound by preconceptions and can see things from the client's point of view. And both NLP and coaching seek to give the client more flexibility, broader 'maps' of who they are, how the world works and what they can achieve.

■ **Mind and body are one system** – The old split between mind and body – which goes back to the seventeenth-century philosopher Descartes ('I think therefore I am') – is a dangerous illusion. Instead, the two are inextricably linked. We can use our physical state, facial expression or posture to directly affect our thoughts and feelings. Many powerful NLP techniques are based on this.

■ **You cannot not communicate** – Whether we want it to or not, our state of mind is expressed in our body posture, facial expression, voice tone (etc.) and will send messages to other people, who will form judgements accordingly.

■ **It is easier to change yourself than others** – As therapist and philosopher Viktor Frankl put it, 'The last of human freedoms is to choose your attitude in any set of circumstances'. When we change our response to other people's behaviour, they seem to change almost miraculously! NLP firmly believes in the principle that people need to take responsibility for their lives and not blame others for their condition.

- **Energy follows intention** – One of Timothy Gallwey's key points was that trying desperately for an 'outcome', such as a better serve, often yields no results, as the 'internal chatter' starts up and the serve actually deteriorates. He suggests a better process: imagine having your desired goal, spend some time really focusing on it, and then leave your unconscious mind to direct your energy and just relax. The result? Success. This model is replicated in NLP.

- **It is often easier to influence through implication than injunction** – An injunction is an order, like a traditional sports coach yelling at someone to watch the ball. People resent being told what to do. NLP coaching is full of techniques for getting round this. Many of these are 'hypnotic' – a term whose meaning will become clear in this book.

- **Clients aren't broken – they work perfectly** – A client who becomes very angry or upset will do so with amazing consistency – i.e. they work perfectly at getting the result, even if those results are not desirable. NLP provides tools to analyse patterns of behaviour and to change those patterns, if the client wishes it.

- **Choice is better than no choice** – (Perhaps not always true in the modern retail environment!) When a client believes they have no choice in a situation, they can become desperate. One of the key roles of coaching is to bring about clients' awareness that they do have choices – including the choice to change themselves. Once a person realises they have choice, this is of itself very empowering and gives a sense of having freedom to act.

- **If you always do what you have always done, you will always get what you have always got** – Although this may again seem obvious, common sense is not always practised, especially in stressful situations, where people often revert to a preprogrammed 'default' response that gets the same old negative result. This presupposition encourages trying something different, the essence of being an effective and flexible human being.

■ **The meaning of the communication is the response it gets** – This is an excellent concept from NLP co-founder John Grinder. It places the responsibility for the communication firmly on the shoulders of the person communicating. If the other person doesn't 'get it', then that means you didn't communicate effectively.

The fit

I hope the above has given a good feel of the spirit and mindset of NLP to anyone unfamiliar with the discipline, and has been a good reminder to NLP-savvy readers. So, what does NLP bring to coaching? The coach faces a number of problems that NLP solves.

■ Coaching has been described as a dance, led by the client. Yet there is not enough material in coaching training on the basic mechanics of this kind of dancing. How exactly do you pick up the lead from the client? Techniques of rapport – especially in their more sophisticated forms – lie at the heart of NLP, and provide clear guidance on this topic. And if, on occasions, the coach needs to lead the client, how is this done in the right spirit? NLP has the answers.

■ A core skill of coaching is to gain an understanding of the client's ' inner world'. NLP provides a way of doing this, without imposing complex and contentious 'big' psychological theories. Instead, it gives the coach detailed tools for observation and for making useful and often powerful deductions from those observations.

- When coach and client see the need for change, NLP provides a huge range of tools to make this happen. Sadly, deep change in human beings is not simply brought about by a realisation of the need for it: people almost always need some kind of process to bring that about. NLP has created, tested and refined a huge number of such processes to cover almost any conceivable coaching requirement. My favourite ones will be covered in Part II of this book.

- The presuppositions contain beliefs that are very helpful for the coach.

Coaching, in return, provides much for the NLP practitioner keen to use his or her skills in a professional context:

- Coaching provides a clear structure for the change process: the form of the sessions, the contract between client and coach, timings, settings and even costs.

- It puts the client at the heart of this process. This is where the client belongs, but sadly NLP is sometimes carried out in a different spirit, where the client has clever things done to them by a charismatic and sometimes aggressive individual. Such fixes are inevitably short-term: lasting change comes from within (encouraged and assisted from outside) rather than being imposed from outside. The coaching framework ensures the client stays in charge.

- It provides professionalism. Coach training and accreditation is a rigorous process and as such provides security for clients and a professional code for coaches.

- Beyond professionalism, coaching provides an ethical framework. Part of the excitement of NLP lies in its decentralised, 'let a hundred flowers bloom' approach – but the catch to this is a lack of an overarching agreement of what constitutes ethical practice. Coaching provides such an agreement.

So - the perfect fit?

Maybe not quite perfect. There are also areas of conflict.

NLP processes are directed. NLP coaches find themselves telling people to do things – 'Put a piece of paper over there, stand on it, imagine a time when you were perfectly happy …' If coaching is an improvised, client-led dance, NLP can be a complex, prearranged ballet, choreographed not by the coach but by the 'big names' of NLP, who have crafted and refined the moves in the light of long experience: the processes are the way they are because they work.

I will show later how this difference can be got round.

At a deeper level, the roles are reversed, with coaching, with its rules and formal accreditation structure, providing the dos and don'ts, and NLP providing the curiosity and experimentation. But I hope that this book will show how these two spirits can reinforce each other rather than clash, and that any tension between them is a creative one.

Cynics say that coaching provides boundaries without depth, and NLP provides depth without boundaries. Fine: let's take the best of both of these, and give our clients (and ourselves) both boundaries and depth. The result, NLP coaching, will be something of great transformative power.

The six levels of coaching

As a coach, you will find yourself working in a range of contexts – with different clients or the same client at different times – from nerves about an upcoming presentation to deep anxiety about the meaning of life. These contexts require different coaching approaches.

Robert Dilts has developed a model for this, called Coach to Awakener. It is based on another NLP model of Robert's called the Logical Levels, which I need to outline first. The Logical Levels is a way of analysing the factors involved in human motivation – and human limitation – into six very different aspects. These are:

- Mission or spirit
- Identity
- Beliefs and values
- Capabilities
- Behaviour
- Environment.

Mission or spirit is our relation to the larger context in which we live. People with a mission dedicate their lives to something that is larger than themselves, to something to which they feel connected and that shapes their view of themselves and guides their decisions. This is clearly a powerful motivator, and lack of mission can be a powerful limiting force on someone.

Identity is 'who we really are'. It is about our boundaries – where we end and the world and other people begin. It's about our deepest 'sense of self', a realisation we first made in infancy, that we are separate individuals needing to survive a whole host of dangers, and that we often spend the rest of our lives making sense of. Identity is precious and often vulnerable but at the same time can be perceived as being set in stone, to a point where people have no notion that it can be changed. People will give up a lot – in the case of martyrs for a cause, everything – rather than face any challenge to their identity.

Beliefs and values are how we decide that something is possible or impossible, important or trivial, worthwhile or reprehensible. *Beliefs* are statements that we think are true but cannot check or haven't bothered to check. Many beliefs are acquired during childhood, either adopting the beliefs of parental figures or based on life as seen by a child. Often when these beliefs are examined by us as adults, they turn out to be wrong. They often take the form of generalisations (all *x*s are *y*) or statements about what is possible or impossible (for us or for 'people' in general).

Values are the key principles that are inherently important to us, such as honesty, compassion and hard work. They can be argued about in words ('Honesty is important, don't you think?'), but their true test is how we feel about them – especially if we have broken the rules they imply.

Our *capabilities* are our skills and knowledge – the ability to speak, walk or read; the ability to write books or to coach with NLP.

Behaviour is about what we actually do, and the habits behind those actions.

Environment refers to the physical contexts within which we act – and are motivated or limited.

In terms of personal growth, development can take place at all of these levels. Many people find it helpful to isolate a level on which they need to progress. Do you need to go on a spiritual retreat or just brush up your sales skills?

Dilts created the Coach to Awakener model by taking the Logical Levels and applying it to coaching. Looking at the different levels ...

Environment

At this level, the coach is a kind of guide. We can point out facts to clients. We can recommend books, websites and courses, and also make introductions.

Sometimes changes to someone's surroundings can be the intervention they need in order to change. For example, a client who said he was depressed spent much time focusing on his beliefs and identity, but it turned out that he was living in a draughty rented room in a broken-down house. I pointed out the effect this was having on him, and he decided to move to somewhere better. The change in his whole character was remarkable.

Behaviour

At this level, the NLP coach acts more like a traditional performance coach. Coaching has many habit-building techniques: examples include reading a book one evening rather than watching TV. Without these, skills (see below) can be abstract and not very helpful. Habit and practice gets them 'in the muscle'.

Goal setting belongs in this category, as does preparing people for difficult situations, walking them through events such as giving a presentation or asking for a date.

Capability

At this level, the coach can be a teacher, providing the client with information and teaching them NLP techniques such as anchoring.

In executive coaching, the coach can also do part of what a consultant does, pointing out relevant business models and helping the client frame their issues in the light of them.

There is, I feel, a dividing line above capabilities. Beyond this, things become much more intense and, as a result, more challenging.

Beliefs and values

Here, the coach can act as a mentor. Mentors are different from teachers: they don't only show you how to do things, but *why*. They can show you the mindsets you need to succeed in your chosen area.

Part of this is done unconsciously: clients will pick up on a good coach's attitudes – and the beliefs and values behind them – without any active 'pushing' of these. But the NLP coach can also actively don their mentoring hat and be explicit about their beliefs and values, especially those most relevant to the client's issues. This is a bit of a departure from the conventional coaching model, but I shall explain later how the two can be squared.

There are many NLP techniques aimed at resolving limiting or conflicting beliefs, some of which we cover in Part II of this book. They can be hugely powerful.

Identity

Dilts calls coaching at this level sponsorship, and observes: 'Sponsorship involves promoting the unique identity of the client'. He goes on to say:

> Sponsorship involves seeking and safeguarding fundamental qualities and potentials within others, and providing the conditions, support and resources that allow that person to express and develop their unique aptitudes and capabilities to the fullest degree.

I find that talking early in the coaching process about coaching at this level often of itself brings about great change in clients. People aren't used to being given this kind of respect, Carl Rogers' 'unconditional positive regard': maybe it is something they have never experienced, even as children.

Coaching at the level of identity can be hugely powerful, but it can also be dangerous. A smooth persona can hide a deeply troubled individual, who may suddenly become disengaged and even aggressive if they feel their identity is under threat. The blander kind of coaching will leave this persona undisturbed (just a bit better organised): coaches may find themselves wandering into this challenging area and need to be prepared.

To coach at this level requires a high level of personal integrity. Gandhi said, 'Be the change you wish to see in the world', and this is the perfect motto for this kind of work. The challenge of becoming ever more such a person is an ennobling and exciting one.

Mission or spirit

The top of the logical levels is that of mission or spirit. Dilts says that at this level the coach is an awakener:

> Awakening others involves supporting them to grow at the level of vision, mission and spirit ... opening up new vistas and possibilities ... and providing contexts and experiences which bring out the best of that person's unawareness of purpose, self and the larger systems to which he or she belongs.

The coach can work with people to help them, or an organisation, develop a sense of purpose and direction.

The coach can also share meditation practices, which provide a method for people to have a very personal 'spiritual' experience. This is sometimes presented as a simple capability, learning a relaxation technique to avoid nervousness in some situations. But I believe it goes much deeper than this. Please note, I have no specific spiritual agenda in saying this: the job of the awakener is to awaken, after which the client will make their own spiritual discoveries if they so wish.

Mindsets and levels

It is worth considering the different mindsets that the coach needs to be in to coach most effectively at the different levels (as you will see in this book, altering your own state in reaction to the state of the client is at the heart of good NLP coaching):

- **Environment** – The mindset for the coach at this level is a practical one.
- **Behaviour** – At this level the coach is like a 'curious student', asking the client to explain to them how they are going to accomplish the tasks that lie ahead.
  - The coach can sometimes morph into a performance coach at this level, helping the client build good habits for themselves.
- **Capability** – The state for the coach at this level is that of teacher of adults, explaining content clearly and using appropriate examples.
- **Beliefs and values** – There are two 'states' necessary here:
  - That of mentor is embodying your own beliefs and values with integrity, as in the Gandhi quote.
  - When working with conflicting or limiting beliefs and values, the coach needs a state of clarity and compassion: this is very sensitive material for the client, and it is important for the coach to respect and honour the client for allowing him or her to be trusted in this fragile area.
- **Identity** – The unconditional positive regard of Rogers: caring for who someone *is* rather than what they do.
- **Spirit or mission** – The awakener holds the excitement and intensity that goes with the realisation of this powerful motivating force.

The Coach to Awakener model provides a unifying methodology for coaching. It has many implications and applications for the coach, which I will attempt to address throughout this book.

Coach to Awakener

Coaching at the level of ...	I act as a(n) ...
Spirit/mission	Awakener
Identity	Sponsor
Beliefs and values	Mentor
Capability	Teacher and/or consultant
Behaviour	Performance coach
Environment	Guide

The sessions

Coaching begins before the client arrives – in Chapter 1, I shall talk about setting up a session, in all ways, from getting the geography of the room right to ensuring that you are in the best possible state to coach. In Chapter 2, I shall take you through an initial coaching session, including a very specific contracting methodology that I created with Hilary Cochrane, my coaching supervisor and one of the finest coaches I have ever met.

In Chapters 3–5, I shall look at what has been going on psychologically during this session and how you can use this to best advantage. Chapter 3 deals specifically with creating the relationship with the client, and Chapters 4 and 5 with ways in which the coach begins to 'map the inner world' of the client.

Chapter 6 looks at subsequent sessions, including the final one. How do you bring the work to the best possible end?

1

PREPARING TO COACH

"There is something I do before I start a session. I let myself know I am enough. Not perfect. Perfect wouldn't be enough. But that I am human, and that is enough. There is nothing this person can say or do or feel that I can't feel myself. I can be with them. I am enough."

Carl Rogers

A coaching session begins before the client appears.

You want to have set up the room well. If this is not a first session, check any notes you made from previous sessions, and remind yourself of the key issues and where the client has 'got to' with them. Most importantly, you want to get into the right state of mind to coach: below I shall talk about intention, quitting your agendas, creating a coaching 'anchor' and meditation – plus a comment on anxiety.

"A coaching session begins before the client appears."

For readers who are not formal coaches but who want to integrate NLP coaching into their lives, the material that follows is still of great importance: getting yourself into the right frame of mind before any potentially challenging encounter is an essential part of living the NLP coaching way.

Getting the room right

Coaching can take place in all kinds of locations. I prefer to take the client away from their usual environment, as this adds to the sense that a special space is being created. But I have coached in people's front rooms (and down the telephone, an increasingly popular coaching medium). In all cases, do whatever you can to ensure the session will not be disturbed.

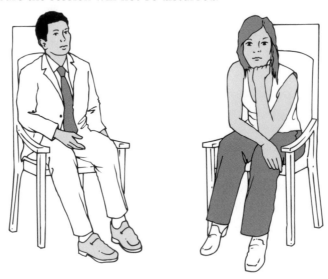

"It is up to the client: if they are unhappy with the arrangement, change it to what puts them at ease."

I find it best to sit next to clients, with our chairs at 45 degrees to each another. This enables us to have a kind of shared space in front of us: clients will often use gestures to draw the future on a kind of imaginary canvas in front of them, for example saying 'I really want to get my business off the ground' and holding out a hand in front of them as they say this. As an NLP coach, I will want to use this space, and will point to it when I refer to the client's business aspirations as the client has unconsciously associated that space with that issue (try it and see!).

I also like to sit to the client's left, as I have found that it is easier if my right ear is closer to them. There is research that shows that the right ear connects directly into the language centre in the left part of our brains.

When I am coaching a female client, they may not feel comfortable if I sit this close to them, so I usually arrange a table where we can sit at right-angles: they sit at the head of a table and I sit to their left.

In the end, of course, it is up to the client: if they are unhappy with the arrangement, change it to what puts them at ease.

Setting an intention

NLP trainer Suzi Smith tells the story of a group of NLP master practitioners who wanted to 'model' a famous shamanic healer. They went all the way to South America to watch him in action. He invited one of the group, who had pains in his stomach, to lie on the floor. He then danced around, singing and pouring various liquids on to the patient. He picked up a range of charms, objects and musical instruments. After about 20 minutes, the man on the floor reported that his stomach felt completely better.

The master practitioners were completely baffled: what did this shaman do? So they started asking all sorts of questions. Was it important that he went clockwise or anticlockwise in his dance? Why did he change direction at a particular point? What was the purpose of the liquids and charms? After a while the shaman began to laugh and said, 'When I want to heal a person, I start with an intent to heal; then I ensure there is a good relationship created between us. All the rest is just ritual.'

To apply this directly to coaching is a bit cynical: I don't think coaching interventions are 'just ritual'. But maybe they are not as important as some coach trainers think. There is a lot of evidence to show that, provided a coach has a set of practices in which they genuinely believe, there is really very little difference between the different schools of coaching: the differences between outcomes actually depend on the individual coaches and the quality of relationship they create with their clients. (For references to this evidence, see the bibliography at the end of the book.) So maybe the shaman wasn't too far off the mark, after all.

So, begin by setting an intention.

I like to spend some time reflecting on the client and get a sense of what is the right state for me for that session. I then generalise this sense by creating a metaphor for it. For example, I may decide that I want to be in flow. I then relax for a few moments and see if something 'pops into my head' – last time I did this, the image of a waterfall came to mind and I used that as a metaphor to set my intention.

Remember the NLP presupposition that 'energy follows intention': once your intention has been set, simply allow your unconscious to get on with it and trust that energy will flow where it is needed without any further conscious effort on your part.

Quitting your own agenda

To coach well it is necessary to suspend your agenda and allow the client's agenda to take over. This is a feature unique to the coaching relationship: most – maybe all – other human interactions involve agendas on both sides.

"To coach well it is necessary to suspend your agenda and allow the client's agenda to take over."

Suspending your agenda(s) is harder than it seems. You need to understand yourself and which agendas you find it hard to give up. Some examples:

- **Wanting to be liked** – Most people who go into coaching (or who want to integrate NLP coaching into their lives) are nice. Which is great – but such people can want, or at least expect, others to like them back in return for being that way. But coaching isn't about being liked, it's about doing a job for the client. Wanting to be liked is a natural human trait, but it's best kept outside the coaching session. This isn't so the coach becomes some kind of bully, but it is so the coach is free to make challenging observations if necessary.

- **Wanting a friend or business partner** – This takes the above desire a step further and gets even more in the way of the coaching relationship.

- **Wanting a relationship or partner** – Clients are often in a vulnerable place and find that the attention of a coach offers something that is missing in their lives. It is, of course, entirely unethical to take advantage of this.

- **Proving your skills** – This is a common agenda for new coaches. I'll talk more about anxiety below; for now, be aware that it's easy to bring this agenda to a coaching session but important not to. This can manifest itself in a feeling that listening isn't enough: suddenly you want to 'wow' the client with some amazing insight or clever technique. But the client probably wants to be listened to more than 'wowed'. Of course, there will be times when the clever technique is right – but that time will emerge from the flow of the interaction with the client. There will also be a time where you try a technique for the first time 'live', not in practice. Applying new techniques lightly and being willing to admit to mistakes makes this acceptable to clients.

- **Needing the 'gig'** – If you coach for a living, and you haven't got a lot of work at the moment, and this is a trial session for a large corporate coaching project …

- **Wanting 'results'** – Some coaches can pressurise clients into making decisions they are not really ready to make, or to make commitments they are not ready to undertake. As with much NLP coaching material, judgement is essential. It is part of your job to gnaw away at blockages in the client, but not to kick them down. Doing the latter may free the client for the moment, but in the long term it does them no favours: as they have not removed the blockage themselves, it will simply reform some time in the future, and they will be as helpless as ever in the face of it.

■ **Wanting to heal yourself** – This is a big one. Everyone on the planet has 'issues' or problems of some kind. Some people are intelligent enough to realise they have these and courageous enough to do something about them. One way is to study coaching. Which is fine, as long as the personal development and the coaching work are kept separate. You are there for the other person, not for your personal growth. I have noticed that clients often bring 'my issues' to me; in other words, the problem they are struggling with is exactly the problem I am facing in my life. I think – ah, maybe they will come up with something that can help me! Usually, they find ways of resolving their issues that have no relevance to me at all: never mind, I have done my job as a coach, which is what matters. At other times the work is directly relevant, such as the time I coached a client with problems about signing a contract under duress, and the following day a famous NLP trainer attempted to do the same thing to me! Here, I treat the learning as a gift and do not let it affect the client's experience in any way.

You do not have to fight the battle against these agendas on your own. Most serious coaches have coaching themselves and also separately have coaching *supervision*, a form of one-to-one advisory service to help resolve practical issues that have arisen within recent coaching sessions. Issues can include where a client is sent against their will or to help delineate the boundaries between coaching and therapy. When starting out, it is best to receive supervision on a monthly basis; later on, when you are more experienced, you can reduce this frequency and see your supervisor when you decide you need to.

Remember the quote 'be the change you wish to see in the world'. If you are having trouble quitting agendas, you are not addressing your own issues. How can a client have faith in you if you are unwilling to make changes yourself?

Even if you are not formally coaching but are simply setting out to live in a new way, you are undertaking a journey, which will probably mean having some kind of coaching or therapy. Much as I'd love it to be, this book on its own will not be enough!

Having an anchor to get into the coaching state

It is useful to have a specific tool you can use to get you into a coaching state: a word, a gesture, a metaphor, a piece of music that 'takes you straight there'. I shall show how you create such a tool in Chapter 8 – the process is called 'anchoring'.

Meditation

You can also do this. I find it a most powerful way of stilling the mind, which otherwise can 'butt in' on a coaching session with internal chatter. Here is a brief, simple meditation exercise I use, that uses the three types of breathing we can do.

Three Tyres meditation and breathing exercise

Start by spending a few minutes simply relaxing and focusing your mind inward. Notice your breathing – what parts of your body move, what parts are touched by the expansion of air in your lungs, and the sense of the internal effect of each breath.

Then ...

▶

1   Imagine there is a tyre, the width of your outstretched little finger to thumb, around your lower belly, sides and lower back (the abdominal region).

2   As you breathe in, imagine this tyre expanding. It may help if you imagine a white mist filling this tyre, or you can focus on the different sounds or sensations of the breath moving in.

3   As you breathe out, imagine this tyre contracting, squeezing out the air around your belly, sides and lower back. As above, it might help if you imagine the mist leaving the tyre, or to focus on the sounds and sensations of exhalation.

4   Stop the visualisation and breathe without trying to change anything; simply observe your breathing. How has it changed from before?

5   Now move the imagined tyre up to your ribcage, and expand and contract it in the same way. Notice the expansion in the ribcage, your sides and back. Then stop the visualisation and breathe without trying to change anything; simply observe your breathing. How has it changed from before?

6   Now move the image of the tyre up to your shoulders, and expand and contract in the same way. Notice how you can also breathe using muscles near your collarbone – this is called clavicular or 'shallow' breathing. Then stop the visualisation and breathe without trying to change anything; simply observe your breathing. How has it changed from before?

7   Starting at the lower part again, breathe in and 'inflate' the lower tyre. Then, still with the same breath, move up and inflate the middle tyre. Then do the same for the top tyre.

8   To exhale, deflate the collarbone tyre, the ribcage tyre and the abdominal tyre in that order.

9   Repeat inhaling and exhaling in this way. Do this at least five times – more if possible. Experienced meditators can slow their breathing right down, taking 60 seconds to inhale and 60 seconds to exhale. Work slowly towards this goal: if it becomes uncomfortable, stop!

10 Stop the visualisation and breathe without trying to change anything. Simply observe your breathing. How has it changed from before?

A comment on anxiety

Coaching is in some ways a performance skill. As for any performance, a measure of anticipatory anxiety is not always a bad thing: it encourages us to learn and develop our skills; it also encourages preparation and readiness.

Of course, excessive anxiety is not good – the meditation material above should help drive that away. But don't view anxiety as an enemy to be fought to the death. Once anxiety is not present at all, it might mean you are no longer taking coaching seriously enough.

All ready to go? You've read your notes and set the room up the way you like. You've set an intention for the session. Maybe you've reminded yourself of those aspects of your own agenda that you've been working on with your own coach and that you are not going to bring into this session. You've done a brief meditation to still mental chatter. Even so, you feel a trace of anxiety, but you remind yourself that this is a good thing, a sign that you care about the quality of your work.

There's a knock on the door. Your client has arrived.

Preparing to coach

- Get the room right
- Set an intention
- Quit your own agenda
- Have an 'anchor'
- Meditation
- Three Tyres
- Accept a little anxiety as part of the experience.

2

CONTRACTING AND THE FIRST SESSION

"An ounce of framing is better than a pound of reframing."

NLP saying, attributed to various trainers

The first session usually lasts two hours. It can be a pretty intense experience. As a result, this will be a long chapter.

"The first session can be a pretty intense experience."

I shall go into the contracting part of the session in particular detail, as it is (a) essential to good NLP coaching and (b) often ignored in books on the subject.

The first session can (roughly – nothing in coaching follows precise rules) be broken down into the following sections:

1 Introduction

2 Contracting

3 Gathering some information

4 Agreeing on the areas of primary focus

5 Doing some actual coaching

6 Closing the session.

Let's look at each of these in turn.

Introduction

The first time I meet a new client, I stand up, look them directly in the eye, shake their hand and introduce myself. Be confident and friendly. It's pleasant to start with a piece of small talk.

> Hi, nice to meet you. I hope you had a good journey here.

Then move on, as quickly as feels right, to your introduction. The main purpose of this is to let the client know they are in safe hands. NLP comes into play at once here: get into rapport with the client and begin to pace and lead them into a relaxed state – I shall show how to do this in the next chapter.

I like to begin by 'introducing the introduction':

> Coaching is mainly about you talking and me asking you questions. However, the first session begins with about 15 minutes of what is called contracting, setting the scene for this and future sessions. Is it OK if I begin, or do you have any questions first?

Usually they agree. I follow this up with:

> May I start by telling you a tiny bit about myself?

The answer has never yet been 'No!'

I only give brief details. I tell them I've been coaching for *x* years, and remind them that I'm qualified with the ICF, the biggest coaching accreditation body in the world. I explain that I have regular supervision, and say a bit about how this works. Then I ask the client if they want to know why I coach. About half of them want to. My reason is that I've learnt that you can both have a successful life and enjoy the journey, and I want to help other people do the same. What's yours?

If you are not qualified, establish credibility another way. Maybe you're working towards qualification: at least the client knows you are on a properly guided track leading towards professional accreditation. If you are unqualified but have many years' experience of coaching, then that can reassure. I then tell the client a bit about coaching and how it works. At this point, we are beginning to move into the next phase of the session, contracting.

Contracting

Contracting is an essential part of coaching, but it is often given insufficient attention in coach training, which often talks about coaching being a designed alliance but doesn't go into sufficient detail about how the alliance actually gets designed. The answer is that this happens in the contracting process, and especially in the contracting that takes place at the start of the first session – though it is essential to understand that contracting is something that continues to happen *throughout* the coaching.

Contracting is particularly important for the NLP coach. NLP stretches the remit of the coach, and to do this you need the wholehearted agreement of the client. Such agreement is achieved with contracting.

There are a number of aspects to contracting: I always bring a list into a first session to make sure I don't miss any out. I shall say a bit about each one, and in Appendix C present a 'script' that you can use – or, better, adapt to suit your own style – to take a client through this process.

1 **Explain what coaching is** – People often have misconceptions about coaching, and it's best to clear them up right at the start. As you do this, you also begin to find out what kind of coaching the client wants (to start with, anyway: clients' wants – and needs – often change as the sessions unfold). I first say a few lines about what coaching is in general, and then introduce (briefly) the Coach to Awakener model.

2 **Confidentiality** – This is, of course, essential to the coaching process. The client must know that whatever they say in the session will be totally confidential, that you will never tell

anybody else about it. If you are doing executive coaching, the confidentiality situation is more complex: whoever is paying for the coaching may want some kind of 'report' from you. I shall deal with this specific issue later.

"The client must know that whatever they say in the session will be totally confidential."

3 **Safety** – I tell clients that I'm unshockable (so far in my coaching life, this has proven to be the case), so they can feel safe to say whatever they like, on whatever topic they like. Of course, you do have to mean this. The client also needs to understand that if a problem emerges that is beyond the scope of the coaching approach, you will refer them to a trusted, competent therapist. Saying this early in the proceedings makes the client feel safer, and also makes such a referral less problematic if it becomes necessary.

4 **Terms, conditions and money** – Coaching is usually given in blocks, often of six sessions. There also needs to be clear agreement about price, cancellation fees and cancellation notice. Common practice is to refund fees if 24 hours' notice is given, but not if notice is given later. New coaches might choose to be flexible here: if a good client forgets to turn up for a session once, you may consider it wisest to use the time doing some admin work and 'let them off' the fee. You may wish to agree a written form of contract with your client.

5 **Style** – I kick off this section with a simple question. 'How do you like to be treated?' This may seem rather obvious – people want to be treated respectfully, surely? – but actually, asking this question can of itself lead to long, revelatory and healing conversations. Some clients are pleasantly surprised and say they have never been asked it before. Others are quite taken aback. The idea of starting a relationship with another individual where you can choose how that relationship operates is unusual and empowering.

The client will usually respond with something about values: typical comments are, 'I want you to be truthful and be straight with me' and 'I like to be treated politely and with respect.'

If a client says something negative, such as 'I don't like it when people are duplicitous and seem to have hidden agendas', repeat that back to them and get them to 'reframe' their statement in a positive form: how they like to be treated. They will then usually look at you quizzically and say 'With openness and respect, obviously.'

NLP Dictionary

Reframing is about getting people to look at things in a new way. All our perceptions are experienced in some kind of context, and if we change the context, the perception – or our reaction to it – can change. A classic reframe is that of a client choosing to no longer see themselves as a victim but as responsible for their life instead.

6 **Challenge and the 'wrong question'** – Two important questions here. First: 'Is it OK if I challenge you?' I have never had a client say 'No' to this, though sometimes they will say 'Yes, as long as you do so respectfully.'

Second: 'Is it OK if I ask you what I call the "wrong question"?' In a well-designed coaching relationship, the coach has permission to ask a 'wrong question' and the client has permission to point out that a question is wrong (i.e. they don't want to answer it). With this permission I feel able to ask any question (if I'm a little doubtful, I can preframe it with 'This may be a wrong question, but …'). This frees up my intuition to come up with good interventions. Without this permission, I can 'lose the moment' worrying about the question. For the client, the freedom to say 'No' to answering a coach's question is another reassurance that they are really in charge of the process.

7 **Optional accountability** – Clients often leave sessions with resolutions. 'I'm going to confront Keith about his rudeness tomorrow!' Traditional coaching practice is to begin the next session by reminding the client of all these resolutions, and asking if they have been carried out. This is called 'holding the client accountable'. In practice, I have found this works for some clients but not others. Some clients like being held accountable – they feel it gives them momentum and direction, and they feel that it shows the coach cares. Others do not: many coaching clients have a task list bulging at the seams, and pressing them to add further deadlines is counterproductive and frankly cruel. However, offering them optional accountability puts them in charge of the process: busy clients can then choose what they want to be held to account for, and not feel ashamed that they haven't fixed everything in their life since the last session.

8 **Taking the learning forward** – Clients need ways of taking what they learn in the session out into their life. Different people have different ways of doing this, such as:

   ■ **Taking notes** – Many clients like to take notes at the end of a session – or half way through, if they feel the need. They need to be told it is OK to do this, otherwise some clients will miss this opportunity as they feel it is rude to interrupt the flow (which it isn't, of course: it's their time). Incidentally, it's much better if clients take their own notes. You will probably want to take your own notes, too, but it doesn't work for clients to use these as substitutes for their own.

   ■ **Regular stopping to reflect on the session so far** – Some people like to flow on for the whole session, while others like to pause and reflect on what has passed in the session so far.

   ■ **A final summary** – Even if there is no time out in mid-session, it is always a good idea to wind matters up a little before the end of the session and to reflect on what has gone on in it. The client needs to agree to this, however.

- **Homework** – Most coaching systems involve some of this, where the client has tasks to do in between sessions. The topic is well covered in other coaching books, such as *Co-Active Coaching* – an NLP 'slant' on it is that arguably the best homework a client can do is to learn some NLP, especially techniques like the Meta Model (see Chapter 5), which will help them become their own coach. In practice, some clients, especially executive coaching clients, can find homework irrelevant (or just not have time for it): don't force it on to people.

It's good to point these options out to clients so they can choose which ones they want to use.

9 **Loss of momentum** – I find it very important to make the client re-contract to do a full set of sessions actually in the coaching session itself. They should have done this before, but there is something special about making that commitment inside the coaching 'space'.

This isn't just so they keep on coughing up the money! Clients can appear to get bogged down but actually be on the verge of making a huge breakthrough. Such breakthroughs usually have two aspects:

- They are incredibly liberating when they happen.
- When they are imminent – when the client knows he or she is going to have to talk about *x* soon – they are scary, and people often put up huge barriers to making them, one of which is appearing to get bored.

Commitment to a fixed number of sessions keeps the client moving through the barriers that often come before a breakthrough.

A fixed number of sessions also sets a stamp of seriousness on the process. Coach and client are now both committed to putting time, effort and (in the client's case) money into the relationship. (If the client is paying for the session themselves, they may be unwilling to commit to a full set of six. And applying too much pressure may make it look as if the coach has the 'needing the gig' agenda. So simply state that this is how you prefer to operate and explain why. If you can end the session by agreeing a time for the next one, the client is now aware of your six-session preference and may well end up sticking to it.)

"Commitment to a fixed number of sessions keeps the client moving through the barriers that often come before a breakthrough."

This marks the end of the contracting section – though the contracting mindset remains for the rest of the coaching process. More contracting will be done: for example, when we start deciding on the Areas of Primary Focus, which is essentially a contract between client and coach to work on certain issues. And remember that *whenever* the coach moves to guide, teacher, consultant, mentor, sponsor or awakener, or leaves the pure coaching model to do an NLP process, a specific agreement to do this is needed – yet more examples of this essential process called contracting.

How long should this have taken? For me it usually takes around 20–30 minutes. Some clients may be itching to go and find this frustrating, but it is essential that the contracting is done fully. Other clients may want to talk and drag things out: the contracting needs to be completed in the first session. If the contracting is not completed properly then, the coaching relationship can go wrong later.

Contracting: a history

I'm so passionate about contracting, and its central role in facilitating full-on NLP coaching, that I want to digress briefly into its history.

Therapy originated with Freud, who was a trained medical doctor. This meant a number of things. It meant that Freud used a diagnostic approach to personal problems – there existed a set of illnesses, and part of the 'analyst's' job was to find out what the patient was suffering from, and then apply the cure appropriate to that illness. Such an approach, of course, leads to labelling – patients become 'depressives' rather than people feeling depressed at a certain time in their lives. This labelling came backed up by the 'expert' status of the doctor/analyst. Patients of such experts weren't supposed to understand the terminology, let alone question it. Any attempt to deny the expertise of the analyst was labelled 'resistance' and held up as proof that the analyst was actually on the right track.

The analyst's perceived expertise rested on two pillars. One was sociological: Dr Freud was a doctor, a respected member of an elite – elites were not generally questioned back in the early and mid-twentieth century. The other was what philosophers call 'epistemological': psychoanalysis was presented to the world as science. The same force that had discovered penicillin and built bridges, steamships and aeroplanes was behind it. This was, of course, nonsense, as has been demonstrated by critics such as the philosopher Karl Popper. (This is not to imply that all psychoanalytic models are false: there is undoubtedly some truth in them. But they are not scientific, as wiser modern analysts admit.)

The patient's role in this 'medicalised' model was passive and powerless.

If you were repelled by the arrogance and pseudo-science of early and mid-twentieth century analysis, the other psychological model favoured by 'experts' was behaviourism. This reduced human motivation to learnt responses to stimuli. This was at least scientific, but its shallow view of human behaviour and motivation made it arguably an even more unattractive option.

▶

In the 1950s, people began to rebel against these approaches. I have already mentioned Carl Rogers. Another rebel was the Canadian therapist Eric Berne. Like Rogers, Berne put the relationship with the client at the heart of the curative process – but unlike Rogers, he created structures within which he believed this relationship would flourish. These were partially theoretical – he developed a number of psychological models, called transactional analysis (TA), and gave them clear, 'user-friendly' names so he could discuss them with clients – and partially negotiated with the client: the contract. Berne called the contract 'an explicit bilateral commitment'.

Explicit – Client and therapist sat down and talked it through at the start of the therapy. No buzzwords were to be used: as in NLP presupposition 14, if the client didn't understand something, it was the therapist's fault. Berne taught his clients the basics of TA.

Bilateral – Therapist and client were viewed as people of equal significance. The contract was between their 'Adult' (conscious, rational) personalities, rather than those aspects of personality that Berne called 'Child' or 'Parent' (by the latter, he meant that part of the personality modelled on the individual's parents, not the individual as a parent themselves).

Starting to learn the client's history

The next part of the coaching session is about obtaining, or at least starting to obtain, a history of the client:

> Before we discuss what you would like to have coaching about, it would be helpful if you would give me a little bit of background about yourself – your life, your work, and the names of any key people in your life that you may refer to in the coaching sessions.

Some clients will move through this entire section very quickly: others will start telling you their life story in minute detail. Ideally, this section lasts about 15 minutes, after which you can bring it to an elegant halt and move on to the next section. But use your judgement: I have coached clients who spend the whole of the rest of the session telling me things, but I felt they needed to do this before they could make progress so I let them do it.

Note that this is an area where coaching adds to NLP. Some NLP coaches tell clients they are only interested in 'process', not 'content', and end up steamrollering over clients who have a powerful need to have their story heard.

NLP Dictionary

NLP makes a distinction between *content*, which is what people say ('I was born in 1963. My family were pretty poor, but we were happy …'), and *process*, which is the way they say it – telltale signs from the client's choice of specific words (= 'language patterns') and body language, about how they 'tick' at a deep level and whether they really believe what they are saying.

As part of this section, it is worth finding out how much experience the client has had with coaching and personal development training. Clients unused to personal development work in general or NLP in particular may need to be led gently into doing NLP processes – though note the word 'may': some people are more adventurous than others. It is a matter of judgement, again: if you force a client to try a process before they are ready, they may resent it, but if you don't take risks with clients and assume they don't have all the resources they need, your coaching can become superficial.

Agreeing on the areas of primary focus

The client is usually in full flow from talking about their life. Time to move on to establishing the specific areas you will be working on.

OK, I would now like to find out what are, say, three to five goals you would like to cover over the coming weeks. It is best if you don't go into too much detail about each one, as our objective now is to come up with a list rather than do any coaching. However, it is worth exploring each area in a little detail, to really clarify what you want to work on. I may interrupt you if I sense we are going into too much detail on any specific subject – that way we can get our list drawn up reasonably quickly. We will probably have time later in this session to really unpack one of these areas.

This section is a little more directive than others, as some chatty clients will require some restraining. Remember, the client can always talk more about the issue when the coaching begins: right now, you want to get a list of key areas within 5–15 minutes. If the client is completely determined to talk about an issue, it is probably best to let them: all you have to do is not really coach them but listen until they have said their bit.

If the client is not clear what they want to work on, you can get them to fill in the Coaching Wheel. This is a standard coaching tool, not an NLP one, but it is useful for the NLP coach. I put a brief description of it in Appendix D.

Doing some actual coaching based on one of their areas of primary focus

To do some actual work on an issue in the first session is a very good thing. It removes any lingering fear the client may have about what is going to happen to them once they actually get stuck into issues. It gets the client's mind into the coachee mindset. It can yield early results, which sells the process to the client, who then goes away thinking 'that coaching stuff is great'. It can yield new insights that you can both ponder between now and the next session. And, given that there may only be six sessions, it's just a good thing to get coaching as soon as possible: most people have plenty of material to cover (even if they enter the coaching room not believing this to be the case).

I almost always kick off with the classic NLP coaching process of the Well-Formed Outcome. I have dedicated a specific chapter in the 'processes' section to it, Chapter 7, and will cover it in detail there.

Closing the session

The clock is showing about ten minutes before the end of the session. Time to start winding things up.

Note that much of the material that follows is applicable to every session, not just this first one.

The summary

If the client agreed to do so in the contracting session, end with a summary. The client should be in control of this process, but you should join in if you feel major parts of the story are being left out. As usual, this needs to be done tactfully.

Remind the client that they can take notes if they want to.

If the client wants to do 'homework', this is the time to set it.

The closing question

Once this is done, ask: 'Is there anything else you want to say to feel complete about this session today?'

If the client says that there is, actually, and starts on a long spiel about something, you need to be a little flexible – but only a little. You do not want a two-hour session to turn into a two-and-a-half-hour one. Long overruns eat away at the boundaries that surround the coaching session: these boundaries are part of what makes it special, a 'magical place'. And, of course, your time is valuable: a point the client needs to take on board (even if you actually have nothing to do for the rest of the day).

Use the pacing and leading techniques I outline in the next chapter. If that fails, interrupt and say 'I really need to get going now; may I suggest we discuss this at the next session.'

Post-session comments

When the session is over, clients will often revert to ordinary conversation. This can be distracting and shouldn't be allowed to go on for more than a couple of minutes, however much you like the client. The coaching relationship is special, and small-talk, even outside formal coaching time, can water it down.

However, the odd off-the-cuff client comment can be very revelatory. If this happens, don't pounce on them. But do say something like: 'That's an interesting comment – I've noted it down and we can look at that in the next session if you want to.'

When it's time to end this brief 'resurfacing' ritual, closing my pad, putting my papers away and standing up usually brings things to a nice conclusion. As does asking: 'So, where are you off to now?'

The first session

- ■ Contracting
  - ■ What coaching is
  - ■ Confidentiality
  - ■ Safety
  - ■ Terms, conditions and money
  - ■ Style
  - ■ Challenges and the 'wrong question'

- Accountability
- Taking learning forward
- Loss of momentum
- Agreeing areas of primary focus
- Starting work
- Closing
  - Summary
  - Closing question
  - Post-session comments.

3

CREATING THE COACHING RELATIONSHIP

"To be trusted is a greater compliment than to be loved."

George MacDonald

I've already said that the quality of the relationship between client and coach is probably the most important single factor in the effectiveness of coaching. It is a very special type of relationship, agenda-free (on behalf of the coach) and respectful. It creates a safe and creative space for the client, where they can look honestly at themselves, experiment with versions of themselves, and, above all (if they want to), change themselves.

Creating and maintaining (or 'holding') this space is *the* great coaching art – and NLP is full of techniques for achieving this, which I shall present in this chapter.

The two most important techniques are rapport and what is called pacing and leading. I shall also discuss the five levels of listening, which is not strictly an NLP concept but is something I find useful, and then conclude with some thoughts on the power of silence.

Rapport

Being able to create relationship with people is partially about your attitude to them: a genuine sense of curiosity and caring for that individual. However, there is also a behavioural component, and that is what we will touch on here.

Watching the great therapists in action, it was noticed that they seemed to adjust their body and voice to match those of the client. NLP describes this as 'meeting the client in their map of the world' and calls the resulting ease felt by the client 'rapport'. It is a technique that can be learnt.

Rapport begins with noticing small aspects of other people's behaviour, such as:

- Posture
- Gestures
- Voice – tone, rhythm, tempo
- Breathing – location and rate
- Eye movements
- Level of eye moisture
- Facial expression
- Skin tone.

Then you copy them. NLP calls this 'matching and mirroring'.

Posture can be copied reasonably closely – outright mimicry is counterproductive, but emulating someone's basic stance is almost always taken in a positive way.

Aspects of *voice* are best copied more indirectly. Some people speak very quickly; others more slowly; some speak in a sing-song accent; others more in a monotone. A gentle altering of your own speech, so that it is more like your client but still essentially 'you', is very powerful.

Transfer the skills you gained by practising the Three Tyres exercise to becoming aware of 'where' and 'how' the other person is *breathing*. You can breathe from the same place (abdomen, ribcage or collarbone) and at a similar rate. Practices such as yoga and qigong are an ideal way to master these skills.

Facial expressions can be matched – again, with subtlety. If someone is smiling, smile. Your smile, not theirs, but a smile nonetheless ...

Watch out for *repeated movements* that people are often making, such as tapping fingers or swinging feet. These can be 'cross-matched', which is basically copying an aspect of their movement with another part of your body. For example, if someone is tapping their left foot, you might begin to tap your right finger in time.

An advanced method of matching and mirroring gestures is called micro-muscle modelling: firing the relevant muscle groups without creating much movement at all. For example, when some-body raises a glass to drink, rather than raise your own glass too, you simply create tension in the relevant muscle groups, reach for your own glass and hold on to it for a while. When the person puts her glass down, you can begin to relax your arm muscles, and when that person lets go of the glass, you can let go of your glass.

The result of good matching and mirroring will be the creation of rapport. This has two benefits. The first is that the client will feel more at ease in your presence; the second is that you may well gain unconscious insight into how the client is feeling and even into what they are thinking. Exactly how this works is a bit mysterious – but try it and you will see it can produce remarkable results.

"The result of good matching and mirroring will be the creation of rapport. The client will feel more at ease in your presence; you may well gain unconscious insight into how the client is feeling."

How do you establish rapport in the first coaching session?

First, set an intention to create rapport with your client before you start.

Then, once they have arrived, keep a look-out for 'cues' in the behavioural areas I mentioned above.

Then match and mirror. This can be done very quickly. You don't need to freeze into a posture that copies the client or mimic their every move. The more skilled at matching and mirroring you become, the faster you are able to click into a matching pose, discretely copy a gesture or assume a voice tone, and then click back to your own style again and fully focus on what the client is actually saying. In the vast majority of cases, rapport will have been established in those few moments.

Learning to match and mirror

To do this well, you first need to become a good observer of people's posture, voice, breathing (etc.). So simply observe and 'notice what you notice'.

As staring at people can be perceived as rude, learn to observe using 'peripheral vision'. Rather than staring at them directly, you can soften your gaze and appear to be looking elsewhere, while actually spotting all sorts of useful information.

Your ability to notice things about the client – in NLP we call this *sensory acuity* – will hugely enhance your ability as a coach.

Then you need to practise matching and mirroring. Do this discretely, obviously in situations that are not hostile: early attempts at matching and mirroring are best made with someone who won't mind too much if they think you are taking the mickey out of them! For example, in a restaurant, try copying someone's hand gestures under a table.

Why does rapport work? The brain is unconsciously always scanning other people, on the look-out for signals of their intent. It does this very fast – consider how quickly you form a first impression of someone (and how accurate this often turns out to be). One of the key mindsets of NLP is awe for the unconscious mind – its speed, its precision, its dogged determination to assist us (even if this gets skewed over time:

hence the need for curative processes). The conscious mind is a relative newcomer; the unconscious mind has been evolving for two hundred million years (longer, if you include the reptilian brain in the story) and has become very good at its job, which is what it always has been: helping us to spot and bond with potential friends and to spot and defend ourselves from potential enemies.

Once back in rapport and listening to the client's content, the skilled NLP coach will still be monitoring the client's signals, keeping half an eye open for significant changes. As with many aspects of coaching, this is a balance you learn to keep.

Pacing and leading

When my children were four or five years old, I used to prepare weekend meals for them. When the meal was ready, I would walk into the living room, switch off the TV and ask them to come and eat. They became upset. After learning NLP, I would go and tell them the dinner will be served in five minutes, at which time I would switch off the TV. When I returned five minutes later they easily accepted this and came to dinner without making any fuss. Obvious? To some, maybe – but I found it a revelation, and one of the most powerful concepts from NLP.

It's called 'pacing and leading'.

You first get yourself into rapport with your client, using the skills above. Then you can lead them somewhere else.

Some may simply refer to this as good manners.

An example of pacing and leading occurs when a client enters a session with an unhelpful level of energy – either agitated or tired and 'shut off'. In the former case, some coaches think 'Great, they're in touch with their feelings; we can really work

Holding the Bird – 'Not too loose; not too tight'

Coaching is about balance and judgement, not perfection.

NLP trainer Stephen Gilligan tells the story of an expert fencer, the actor Errol Flynn, who said that the most important thing was not to hold the sword too tight or too loose. It was a bit like holding a bird, he said: if you hold the bird too tight, you will crush it; if you hold it too loose, it will fly away.

Although this seems an obvious metaphor, I find it one of the wisest principles in coaching (or any activity in life, actually).

on stuff'. But actually agitation is not a good state in which to be coached. It is much better to pace and lead clients to a level where they are open and receptive, and more deeply in tune with themselves and open to new ideas.

You can use the skills you acquired in the Three Tyres exercise to do this, as breathing higher up tends to increase energy, while breathing lower down (abdominally) tends to have the opposite effect.

If the client is overenergised, use clavicular (collarbone) breathing and increase your own energy level until you feel a sense of connection with the client. Don't increase your energy level beyond that of the client: stay slightly below it. This is the pacing. Once you feel connected, slow your breathing and move it 'down': begin breathing in your ribs and then abdominally. As you do this you will notice that your client will gradually breathe more slowly and their state will begin to change. This is the leading.

If the client is at a low energy level, lower your own energy level and breathe abdominally, pacing yourself to connect with the client. Again, once a felt sense of connection happens, you can start to lead, increasing your breathing rate and moving your breathing up to your ribcage.

Many clients who have NLP coaching report that it makes them 'energised': sometimes this can be simply because good interaction has taken place, but often it is because the coach has deliberately paced and led them to that state.

Pacing and leading is a core NLP coaching skill that you can use all through the coaching session, effectively managing the client's state.

The five levels of listening

Listening skills are covered in many coaching books, and so I do not want to go into these in great detail here. But American writer Stephen Covey has a particular take on this topic that I find especially helpful, so I would like to share that. He talks about five levels of listening:

1 Ignoring

2 Selective listening

3 Waiting to talk

4 Attentive listening

5 Empathic listening.

Ignoring is the lowest level. Anyone intelligent and sensitive enough to be reading this book is unlikely to deliberately ignore someone they should be listening to. But we can send out the wrong signals, so that the other person *thinks* we are ignoring them. Unskilled listeners who are unaware of the impact of non-verbal communication may be listening to someone, but their posture, facial expressions, gestures and where their eyes are focused can send the opposite message. Remember some basic signals you can send to someone to say 'I'm listening':

- Nods at appropriate points

- Making eye contact at regular intervals

- Basic matching of their expressions – if they are smiling, smile back.

Selective listening is where we listen to a certain amount of the other person's words hoping to give the impression that we are listening to them all – when we are actually preoccupied with something else. This is not hugely polite, but we all do it from time to time. But not when coaching.

Waiting to talk – we are often in a conversation, and someone has said something that sparks off a response in us. We just have to say our piece! But the other person is still talking. We are now engaged in the conversation, but not in what is actually being said right now. People in this state often look impatient, maybe tapping their fingers or making other staccato movements.

Such behaviour is common in business meetings, or other situations where a measure of aggression is expected. It is not the approach of a coach, however. If the client is in full flow, it is invariably better to let them go with that flow. Acquire the skill of remembering what it was you suddenly 'had' to say and waiting till there's a break in the flow to say it. If it is still appropriate – things may have moved on – introduce it with something like: 'It occurred to me while you were speaking, that …'

An *attentive listener* is a skilled listener. Skilled listening involves doing things such as:

- Getting the basics of nodding and eye contact right
- Matching and mirroring elegantly and subtly
- Making sure you have got the key points of what the client is saying by feeding back their comments to them, via interjections such as: 'Let me see if I understand what you are saying: you want *x* …' or 'So, you want *x* …' Repeating back the exact words of the client is a refinement of this skill. I recently repeated back a word, 'understood', and the client corrected me: 'No, I said understanding.'

This is good listening – but not necessarily quite good enough for good-quality coaching. This is because the above techniques are techniques, and someone who has learnt them can trot them out easily.

Really good listening is … *empathic listening*. In this situation, the listener has all the skills of the attentive listener but adds important additional qualities, of sincerity, genuine interest in and curiosity about the talker. Empathic listening includes the ability to suspend judgement and simply enter the world of the speaker.

Remember the NLP presupposition that energy follows intention; if you have an intention to genuinely listen to a client and care for them, empathic listening should come easily to you.

"Empathic listening includes the ability to suspend judgement and simply enter the world of the speaker."

The value of silence

Many people are uncomfortable with silence. We are taught that we should be 'good' conversationalists, and that if silence falls over a conversation something has gone wrong and we need to get it going again. But actually periods of silence can be of huge value to a client. Sometimes simply sitting quietly with someone while they ponder an issue or make a decision is the best gift you can give them. By staying silent, you are giving them permission, rarely granted in today's busy world, to take time over something.

The way I handle this is simply to say to myself that I will let the other person speak first and see what happens. Being comfortable sitting in silence with someone is a profound coaching skill. It is actually one I learnt in business, long before I took up coaching, where when closing a sale the best thing to do is often to stay quiet and let the customer decide on their own.

However, silence can also be intimidating, so being aware of and understanding the client's response to silence are important. If you have the right level of trust with them, they will be comfortable to sit quietly working things out, without needing to engage with you again until they are ready. This is all about setting yourself out as a 'servant of the client': they do not need to amuse you or keep your attention; it is their time.

All the above techniques – rapport, pacing and leading, empathic listening and skilled use of silence – are key to creating and maintaining the safe, creative space I mentioned at the start of the chapter. You can add further to the power of this space by learning more about the client's inner world and acting elegantly on that knowledge. I shall present some ways to do this in the next chapter.

Creating the coaching relationship

- Rapport
    - Matching and mirroring
- Pacing and leading
- The five levels of listening
    - Ignoring
    - Selective listening
    - Waiting to talk
    - Attentive listening
    - Empathic listening
- The value of silence.

4

MAPPING THE CLIENT'S INNER WORLD

"I speak two languages, English and body."

Mae West, movie star

For the NLP coach, learning about the client isn't only a matter of listening to the content of what they say but in looking at how they say it (process) and what that tells you about them at a deeper level. This chapter will present the main ways of observing process and learning from it.

You begin to notice things about a client at once, of course. Then the 'tell me about yourself' part of the initial session gives you your first big opportunity to look deeper. This chapter will show you some NLP tools for doing this.

You will, of course, be able to continue this learning process throughout the coaching.

Note also that the concepts and tools presented here will be needed for doing the processes in Part II.

States, calibration and congruence

A *state* in NLP is any condition of mind and body. In common speech 'being in a state' means being overwrought, but in NLP a state can be anything from fury to calmness, from terror to quietly getting on with a task.

Many of us have a *default state*, a mental and physical condition we naturally slip into when external pressures are removed. Exactly what this state is differs from individual to individual.

We also have common states that we get into when pressure is applied to us, and one of the jobs of an NLP coach is to help clients alter these states if they are unhelpful to them.

As coaches, we need to learn about the states of our clients, in order to help them change, and also to ensure that they are getting full value from the various NLP processes we use with them. We do this by what NLP calls *calibrating* them. This is essentially compiling and then using a dictionary of that person's inner states and how they express them physically on the outside.

When calibrating, the first step is to notice a set of reactions (posture, expression, breathing, etc.) and then establish what they mean for the client. For example, if someone looks happy, you can ask whether they in fact have the experience of 'happiness' right now. If they say 'Yes', you now know what 'happy' is in that person's body language. Perhaps the corners of their mouth have lifted in a smile; you may also observe a lighter skin tone, wrinkles around the eyes, slower breathing, less strain in the voice, a more relaxed posture ...

This checking can also be done more discretely by noticing someone's expressions, gestures, voice tone (etc.) during a conversation and comparing these with the emotions they are expressing. The coach can sit silently while the client talks and take 'snapshots' of their body and voice tone where the content is obviously happy, snapshots of when they are conflicted, snapshots of when they are stressed, embarrassed (etc.) The coach then has a type of second language beyond what the client is saying. (This is probably done unconsciously by people anyway: calibration makes this skill explicit.)

One thing you are looking to calibrate (in the second sense of the word, working out their state) is *congruence*, or its opposite, *incongruence*.

NLP Dictionary

The word *calibration* is used in two slightly different senses in NLP. The first sense is compiling the 'dictionary' of someone's body language. The second one is using that dictionary to work out what state a client is in. Descriptions of NLP processes will often include the coach saying 'I'm calibrating the client', by which the coach usually means the second meaning: 'I'm looking at the client and working out what they are really feeling or thinking.'

When someone says they want to do something and they really mean it, they are congruent. Their words, body language and voice tone all align. When they say they want to do something, and there is some mismatch between their words and their body language or voice tone, this is a sign that at least some part of them is not happy with what they say – in other words, they are incongruent.

Simply spotting incongruence in a client can be of enormous help to them. I have often spotted incongruence, pointed it out to a client and had them say something like: 'You know – you're right. I'm not that happy about doing *x* after all. That's amazing …'

"Simply spotting incongruence in a client can be of enormous help to them."

The ability to spot incongruence is essential for guiding clients through NLP processes. Many of these involve taking a client from one state, usually an unhelpful or negative one, to another, more positive or 'resourceful' one. To start such a process, we need to be sure that the client is truly in the state they want to change. And at the end of the process, we need to know that it has worked. Clients often want to please, or want a process to have worked when it hasn't, so they will not be always honest about their state after a piece of change work. 'Yes, the problem has gone now', they say, while their body language is largely unchanged from when the exercise began – their shoulders droop, although a little less than when they started; their eyes are still turned down; their skin remains grey ...

We also need to know when we are being congruent ourselves. Think back to when you were wholehearted about something – head, heart and gut all shouting 'Yes' to it. Revisit that moment, now. Remember what you saw at that time, what you heard, what you felt. That is congruence, and you can use that as a model for checking your congruence on future occasions.

Now consider a time when you were pulled in different directions. Maybe you 'thought' something was right but you felt it was wrong ... Revisit that moment, too, and remember the sights, sounds and feelings that go with it. That is incongruence, and it can be your model for that in the future.

Clients can learn to calibrate themselves for congruence or incongruence. This can be a hugely useful tool in decision-making: a decision about which you are congruent is usually a good one. (I cover this material in more depth in my book *Brilliant Decision Making*.)

Rep systems: does the client see, hear or feel?

We acquire information through our five senses. We store it and recall it that way, too: memories are 'made of' sights, sounds, feelings, smells, tastes. Often, a 'trigger' from one sense will bring back a memory laden with the other four. The hero of Marcel Proust's *In Search of Lost Time* dips a madeleine cake in some tea and remembers enough to fill seven novels!

Although we use all our senses, we very often have a 'preferred' sense (not preferred by conscious choice, but one we happen to use more). This preference governs what we notice, what we store in our memory and how we recall it. For most people, the preferred sense is either sight, sound or feel (feel in the broader sense of not only touch but also internal sensations) – Proust's taste preference is unusual.

NLP Dictionary

NLP stresses the similarities between the brain and a computer. Each sense is a *representational system* (or *rep system*) – a way of inputting, coding and recalling information. The five systems are *visual*, *auditory*, *kinaesthetic* (feel), *olfactory* (smell) and *gustatory* (taste). So someone with an auditory rep system is someone sensitive to, and good at remembering, sounds.

NLP uses the acronym *VAKOG* to refer to the five senses.

Our sense preference is reflected in the words we use. People say things like: 'I see your point of view', 'I hear what you're saying' and 'I get it' to express much the same sentiment, depending on whether they have visual, auditory or kinaesthetic preferences.

If you want to engage with someone, it is important to ensure that your communication matches their rep system preference. If you do not do this, the person may well ignore, or at least pay minimal attention to, your input; or if you do get through, your communication is less likely to be worked on internally or even remembered.

The most basic way of matching a sense preference is to use appropriate words. Should the client 'be on the look-out' for something, 'listen out' for it or 'keep up their guard'?

Beyond this, people with a visual preference respond well to gestures, or charts and diagrams. Those with an auditory preference just like to talk and often listen with their eyes closed. And those with a kinaesthetic preference need to make an emotional connection or have a go with something before they really 'process' it.

Students on beginners NLP courses often learn this information and then go round trying to classify everyone into visual, auditory or kinaesthetic. Sadly, life isn't this simple. Most of us use all three – even all five – and many of us do so in a reasonable balance. But there are a number of individuals who are strongly biased towards one sense. These are the ones you have to notice and adapt your communication style for.

The main way to check a client's preference is to monitor their vocabulary.

You can also look at their eye movements to see how they recall information. More on this in the next section.

A final point on rep systems – what is *your* preferred system, and how strong is your preference?

If you have a strong preference for one system, this will affect how you communicate with others (or fail to communicate with them). The stronger your own preference, the more conscious effort you will have to make to communicate in a balanced way, especially when faced with someone with a different strong preference. One of the benefits of studying this material in more detail is that you will be able to improve your ability in other rep systems and thereby keep better rapport with clients who have different rep system preferences from your own.

"The stronger your own preference, the more conscious effort you will have to make to communicate in a balanced way, especially when faced with someone with a different strong preference."

If you work with groups of people, the above material means that you have to mix the senses. Writers, and poets in particular, have known this for centuries. So talk clearly, but also use gestures, or even charts or slides if appropriate.

Digital – a sixth sense?

Another rep system worth mentioning is that which NLP calls 'digital'. In our modern world, many people have become used to acquiring information via written words or numbers. While in a way this is a subset of the other systems, it does seem to have acquired a life of its own as a rep system. I have heard many people say, 'I need to see it written down before I can understand it' or 'The numbers will give a better sense of how this really works'.

People with this preference need to be spoken to in abstract terms – initially at least. Underneath their digital mindset, they will probably also use a preferred sensory rep system: you can pace and lead them into this.

In the business and organisational world, the use of management-speak is very common. A coach working in this area may need to understand these terms (or at least not laugh at them) if they are to seem credible to their clients.

Eye accessing cues

The eye forms part of the central nervous system and develops from the same tissues as the brain, so we can say scientifically that the eyes are an extension of the brain that sits on the surface of the body. As such, they might be expected to give us information about what is going on in the brain, and NLP has shown this to be the case. From looking at people's eye movements you can tell what kind of mental experience they are having. More specifically, these *accessing cues* are:

Eyes up and left (*their* left, not 'left as you see them') – The person is remembering visual images.

Eyes up and right – The person is imagining visually, making up images or fantasising.

Eyes to the side, left – They are remembering sounds or words. Maybe they have a 'tape loop' running in their head …

Eyes to the side, right – They are constructing sounds or words.

Eyes down and left – Internal dialogue is going on.

Eyes down and right – Feelings, both external (tactile) and internal (visceral).

Eyes straight ahead, but unfocused or dilated – Quick access of sensory information (can be any rep system, but is often visual).

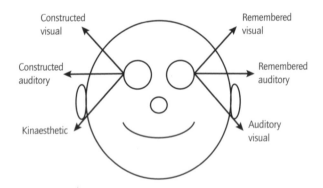

Note that left-handed people often have a reverse pattern to the cues above, e.g. look up and right to remember a picture and look up and left to imagine a picture.

Spend some time practising the above by noticing people's eye movements when they speak. You can also do this by watching television with the sound switched off.

When I ask a client the question 'Where do you see yourself in five years' time?', the question is quite literal: the client needs to imagine a picture of themselves in the future (so their eyes should look up and right). If the client seems confused with this question and is looking elsewhere, I will gesture my hand to a place above and to the right of them, to lead them into the most helpful state of mind. For example:

Coach: Where do you see yourself in five years' time?
Client: [*Looking down left then right*] I … I really don't know …
Coach: [*Pauses, then gestures up to the client's right*] Where do you see yourself in five years' time?
Client: [*Looking up right and smiling*] Running the south-east region.

I would do this even if the client had a non-visual preference. Different senses are better suited for different situations. To gain an overview and clarity (notice these words are visual) requires the use of the client's visual cortex. To get a precise under-standing of what it would actually be like doing something, it is best for the client to look down right and actually experience the sensation. When asking a client to identify potential problems, the client will often look for an answer by looking for words, looking sideways if they just hear a voice or down left if they engage with it.

Strategies

When I asked one of the best coaches I know, Ann Baldwin, what she found most useful from NLP in her coaching work, she said 'Strategies'.

NLP provides a unique glimpse into the precise mental pat-terns people use to accomplish things: modelling the 'success strategies' of highly effective people was how the discipline began. It also shows how people can use a similar set of patterns to *disempower* themselves in a predictable way (remember Presupposition 11, 'People work perfectly').

A good way to understand this topic is to consider that when someone asks us 'How do you do *x*?', we often don't know. 'I've no idea. I just do it!' is a common reply. But careful questioning can reveal a set of mental steps, often surprisingly fast and complex. These sets of steps will have a structure, a regular repeatable form. They are effectively little computer programs that we run in our minds in specific situations. They are sequences of moments of attention we pay to one or other of the rep systems – they are made up of internal pictures, words, sounds and feelings.

An example will make this clear. When choosing a place to go out and eat, I run an internal programme – my strategy. First I pay attention to feelings in my body and I then imagine the choices of food available. Then I imagine the context (time available, cost, company) and imagine how I'll feel after eating the meal. If I imagine I'll feel heavy or sickly after eating, or perhaps still hungry, I'll change my choice until I find something that'll leave me feeling both good and replete. To exit this process, I tell myself 'I'm having *x*'.

In NLP terms:

1 I feel something internally – hunger!
2 I visually imagine the choice of foods available, and the context in which the meal will be taking place.
3 Back to internal feeling – how will I feel after the meal? Good?
4 A little piece of internal dialogue.

Note the link to the eye accessing cues in the previous section. During the running of this programme, an observer would see my eyes go down/right (feeling hungry), move up/right (imagining options), move back down/right (feelings after the meal), and then move down/left (internal dialogue).

Strategies and coaching

For the coach, understanding strategies brings two benefits:

If the outcome of the strategy is negative, you can find (or help the client find) ways of breaking the 'pattern'.

If the strategy is effective, it can be used in other situations where the client currently doesn't have a useful strategy.

It might seem odd to talk of having a strategy for a negative outcome, but we all do this. Consider these two examples that a client may turn out to run:

- **The sadness strategy** – They look down/left and say to themselves 'Life is tough.' Then they look up/right and see dark foreboding images, and then look down/right and notice unpleasant sensations in their body. Then they repeat this, many times.

- **The jealousy strategy** – They look up/right and imagine their loved one in a compromising position with a stranger. Then they look to the side/right and imagine the loved one saying something negative about them. Then they look down/right, feel angry and humiliated, and then look down/left and say: 'This is wrong. They will pay.' Repeat.

These, or variations on these themes, are very common. Note that in neither strategy is there an exit. The 'strategist' just loops round and round. How often do we hear people complaining of being 'stuck' in a mood of some kind?

To help a client break the pattern, we need to help them elicit the pattern and then work with them to identify a way of interrupting the loop.

Here is an example in action:

Coach: How do you know you are experiencing sadness?
Client: I just know.

Coach: Yes ... However, something is going on inside of you when you get this feeling. Where do you actually feel it in your body?

Client: I feel it in my chest. [*Client looks down and to the right*]

Coach: Do you say anything to yourself?

Client: No.

Coach: If you did, what would you say?

Client: I need some space ... Actually, I do say that. Wow! [*Client looks down and left*]

Coach: Are there any pictures?

Client: No, none.

The coach notices the client didn't look up at all: this client's strategy for sadness is therefore: 1. Look down/right and feel pain in the chest. 2. Look down/left and say, 'I need some space'. 3. Repeat.

Explaining this process to clients provides them with choice:

Coach: Is there a way of changing this pattern?

Client: I am not sure how.

Coach: You didn't see any other possibilities?

Client: I could imagine actually doing something.

Coach: Great! What could you imagine doing?

Client: Seeing myself walking in the country near where I grew up.

Coach: Try it.

Client: OK. [*The client looks up/left, recalling a memory of a country walk; the client smiles and sighs*] [*The client looks down/right, shrugs his shoulders and then smiles*]

Client: That's amazing, I feel much better – how weird.

Coach: You've been NLPed!

Metaprogrammes

Different people respond to different types of information and challenge. The underlying cause of this difference is that people have what NLP calls differing *metaprogrammes*, patterns of seeing and reacting to the world that seem to be either innate or built into us at an early age.

As a coach, it is important to identify your own metaprogrammes and those of your clients. This will enable you to enter the client's world and to use language that matches the client's experience.

Many of these metaprogrammes have been identified: here are the most common and powerful ones.

Toward/away from

Some people are motivated to move towards goals, others by the desire to avoid problems or escape an unpleasant past. 'Toward' people are the former. Good at establishing and meeting goals, they can however be seen as naive, as they often overlook problems in the way. 'Away from' people are the latter, good at spotting potential problems and fixing them, though they are sometimes seen as cynical by goal-driven 'toward' people.

"Some people are motivated to move towards goals, others by the desire to avoid problems or escape an unpleasant past."

Certain professions tend to attract people with similar metaprogrammes. For example, solicitors, accountants and doctors are 'away from', while sales and marketing people, politicians, artists and athletes tend to focus on what they want to get – 'toward'.

Ask someone 'What is important about ...', and they will usually reveal their preference, saying something like 'I must make sure it doesn't go wrong' (away from) or 'I must achieve the following' (toward). It is also worth calibrating their body language: are they pointing to some future goal in front of them (toward), or gesturing to stop with palms up (away from)?

Once you notice a client's metaprogramme, you can phrase your questions appropriately. Notice the difference between 'What do you want to achieve?' and 'What will be the consequences if you don't take this action?'

External/internal

To discover this pattern, ask, 'How do you know if you have done a good job?' If the client says 'I like acknowledgement or praise', they have an external pattern. Someone with an 'internal' pattern would say 'I just know'.

An external person will be influenced by strong, fact-based authoritative language, ('Studies have shown ...'). An internal person will also take in data, but they will decide for themselves.

This can be very useful in coaching, as once a client is aware of their pattern, they can understand how it affects their relationships. For example, an internal pattern boss may rarely or never praise staff, because such praise doesn't matter to them. But staff with an external pattern will probably resent this. On the other hand, staff with an internal pattern may find praise patronising.

Options/procedures

Options people are interested in new ways of doing things. They love to create new procedures but find it hard to follow them – they'd rather tinker with them. They are the 'starters'. Procedures people like to follow set patterns and focus on results. They are the 'completer/finishers'.

Ask your client, 'Why did you choose your current job?' If the client answers the question directly with various reasons,

'Location, reputation, opportunity, etc.', they have an options pattern.

A procedures client will actually hear a different question: 'How did you choose your current job?' They will answer with a story or process: 'I came for the interview, I made up my mind and started three years ago (and so on).'

Be aware of your own pattern. If you have a liking for process, you may relentlessly take clients through NLP processes, when more flexibility and listening would yield better results. Alternatively, if you are an 'options' person, you may be tempted to constantly experiment with clients and not give them the benefit of skills you have already mastered but got bored with using.

Sameness/difference (or sort by same/sort by different)

When asked to compare things, 'sameness' people look for the similarities between things and 'difference' people look for the differences. This also extends to how they like things to be: 'same' people, perhaps rather unsurprisingly, don't like change, while 'different' people not only like it but need it.

There is a kind of intermediate programme in between these two opposites, called 'sameness with exception', whereby people like periods of stability punctuated by episodes of change, around every five or seven years.

Ask, 'What is the relationship between your work this year and last year?' Someone with a 'sameness' pattern will answer that things are the same. Someone with a 'sameness with exception' pattern will answer that things are similar but have changed incrementally. Someone with a 'difference' pattern will ignore the question and point out the differences.

As a coach, notice your own pattern. Many coaches have a 'sort by difference' pattern: they chose to leave their careers and to do something radically different, something that involves constant change. That may also bias coaches to encourage change, when 'doing nothing' might in fact be the best course for a particular client to follow at a particular time.

Big chunk/small chunk (general/specific)

'Small chunk' people like detail: at worst, they form no over-view. 'Big chunk' people like the big picture and become impatient with detail very quickly. 'Small chunk' people make good lawyers but poor legal theorists.

There is no specific question for this category: just listen to the level of detail your client gives. A 'big chunk' person may describe a recent holiday as 'great' while a 'small chunk' person is likely to spend ten minutes telling you about their experience.

Coaches with a 'small chunk' pattern often favour encouraging the client to agree to detailed lists of small actions: 'Let's agree five things you can do between now and our next session …'

Coaches with a 'big chunk' pattern often favour encouraging the client to focus on the meaning of life, with little time spent on how to actually implement any change.

Generally speaking, the job of a coach is to encourage clients to do both – to 'chunk up', get a clear big picture of the bigger context in which they are trying to achieve something, and then 'chunk down' and put together a realistic plan, with coherent steps to achieve it. The Creativity process in Chapter 11 is an ideal way to do this.

A great chunking up question is: 'And what would that do for you?'

To get clients to chunk down, ask: 'What is the first step?'

Clients need both big and small chunk thinking. 'Vision without action is a daydream; action without vision is a nightmare', as the Japanese proverb has it.

Self/other (or sort by self/sort by other)

When under stress, some people will tend to focus first on themselves and how a goal will impact on them, while others focus initially on how it will affect other people.

As with chunking, there is no magic question to establish this.

Coaching is very focused on personal development, on how you can get what you want in life: this can be rather self-centred, 'sort by self' material. So coaching arguably assumes a 'sort by self' pattern for the client. Clients who 'sort by others' may find the process uncomfortable at first – especially if they have been sent to you via an executive coaching programme. But it is these people who often end up benefiting the most: persevere.

As a coach, if you have a strong 'sort by self' pattern you may find it difficult to really care about your clients. If you have a strong 'sort by other' pattern, you may feel that self-sorting clients are selfish and therefore unworthy of your time.

Conclusion

Most people will have one or a few dominant metaprogrammes and be more towards the middle in others. Shelle Rose Charvet, author of the classic work on these, *Words that Change Minds*, cites Margaret Thatcher as someone with a hugely dominant internal metaprogramme: when outvoted 49 : 1 on an issue, she said she felt sorry for the other 49. No use telling her that other people didn't agree with her point of view.

The dominant ones are the ones that matter.

Once you have established whether the client has one or several strong metaprogrammes, good coaching will often involve encouraging them to think or act from the opposing preference. 'Toward' clients often need to anticipate potential difficulties more, while 'away from' clients need to create clear goals. 'Options' people need to work more consistently, and 'procedures' people need ways of keying into their creativity (everybody has creativity). Internally referenced people need to consider external evidence more carefully, and externally referenced people need to develop greater belief in their own judgement. The 'big chunker' may get caught out by detail, and the 'small chunker' may miss the big, unstated truth, the 'elephant in the room'. 'Sort by selfers' will get lasting results if they value – and are seen to value – others and their contributions; 'sort by other' people need to value themselves and their contributions more.

From all of the above, the client will benefit from a wider vision of the world and see just how different we all are.

Finally, a word of caution. This material is the NLP equivalent of profiling: defining a person by a number of different criteria. But human beings are always more complex than any theoretical boxes that psychologists create for them. As the great humanist Abraham Maslow said: 'He that is good with a hammer sees the whole world as a nail.'

Arguably, the purpose of much NLP coaching – the Meta Model that follows in the next chapter, for example – is to help people get themselves out of various boxes, boxes they have either been unconsciously influenced into or have put themselves inside for some reason. We do clients no favours by replacing these boxes with new ones.

Representing time and space

Here is another advanced calibration skill that can provide amazingly powerful coaching interventions.

Ask a client to close their eyes and get a sense of events happening in the future. Then ask them to raise a finger and point to that future, and they will do so, usually but not always pointing forward. (Of the thousands of people I have presented this idea to, I have never found a person who was unable to do this.) This is also true of the past: the person usually points in the opposite direction to the future, but, again, not always.

You can extend this to create *timelines* along which clients will arrange their memories and their aspirations and that they can use to imaginatively move into their past or their future.

Voices or 'parts' of someone's personality often inhabit a particular *space*, too. Here's an example.

Client: I see myself as being a partner in the firm. [*Eyes looking up right; gesturing ahead; firm and authoritative voice tone*] But, you know, I can't be arsed. [*Hand gesture of fingers and thumbs in a beak-like structure near left shoulder; critical, cynical voice*]

Coach: May I stop you there? You say you see yourself as being a partner in the firm [*Coach points to the location in front to the right*] but you also say you can't be arsed.' [*Coach points to left shoulder*]

Client: Yes, I know that is strange. [*Blushing*]

Coach: And what is that? [*Pointing to the client's left shoulder*]

Client: Oh my god! What is it? [*Client looks at parrot-like gesture on left shoulder and appears dazed*]

The coach's job is to hold up a mirror to clients and allow them to see things they haven't noticed before – after which clients can make their own judgements.

Conclusion

There has been a great deal of material in this chapter. People new to NLP coaching often look at it all and think: 'I can't look out for *all* this stuff in the early part of a coaching session. I probably can't map it all out in six sessions, let alone one. And at the same time, I am supposed to be listening to the content of what the client is saying, and getting familiar with all that … This is just all too much!'

And, of course, it is. What happens is that if you practise working with these six concepts:

- calibrating congruence and incongruence
- rep systems
- eye accessing cues
- strategies
- metaprogrammes
- representing time and space,

the practice becomes automatic and you just start noticing them. As with most skills, there is no shortcut. Understanding the concepts and how they work will help you, but in the end there is no substitute for getting out there and using this material in real-life situations.

I suggest you practise it in bits. Immerse yourself in rep systems for a while, then concentrate on metaprogrammes, and then look for congruence and incongruence. At all times, stay curious – what's really going on here? This can make the most boring encounters fun – though beware of totally ignoring the 'content' of what someone is saying, which may also be considered rude! Such situations don't have to be therapeutic or managerial: just listen to people you meet in everyday life and look for the signals.

And remember that, when you do use this material in the coaching situation, you are not trying to be perfect. The map you are drawing of your client's inner landscape is not one of those high-definition, tiny-scale ones that includes every field boundary and outbuilding. What you are after are the salient points, the big features – a strong rep system preference, the most powerful metaprogrammes, a few common states (especially ones that disturb and their opposites, the states of congruent happiness).

Mapping the inner world of the client

■ States, calibration and congruence
■ Rep systems
    ■ Visual, auditory, kinaesthetic, olfactory and gustatory
    ■ Digital
■ Eye accessing cues
■ Strategies
■ Metaprogrammes
    ■ Toward/away from
    ■ External/internal
    ■ Options/procedures
    ■ Same/different
    ■ Big chunk/small chunk
    ■ Sort by self/sort by other
■ Representing time and space.

5

QUESTIONS THAT CHANGE BELIEFS

"Common sense is the collection of prejudices acquired by age eighteen."

Albert Einstein

This chapter covers one of the most powerful tools for NLP coaches, the Meta Model. This gives the coach a comprehensive questioning methodology: the client uses specific words that alert you to the possibility of a limiting belief that they hold about themselves or the world, and you have a range of questions you can use to challenge that belief.

Using this model effectively and easily, you can learn a huge amount about the client and – most important of all – help the client rid themselves of all kinds of unhelpful ideas.

To make sense of the model, let's take a step back and consider how we process information.

As children (and adults!) we need to make sense of the world. We are also bombarded with information from that world all the time. What do we do about this?

First, we filter the information as it comes in, simply *deleting* information so we can reduce the flow to manageable proportions. This is something we learn as infants and that we do at an unconscious level.

Second, we *generalise* on information, inferring general principles from recurring events. Watch a baby drop something out of their pram over and over again: the baby is finding out whether the pattern is consistent – does it always go down? Babies discovered gravity, not Newton! As we grow older, we find this useful as a learning mechanism: once you learnt to use one door key, you could use any key. However, generalisations also have negative consequences, such as prejudice and pessimism.

We also play with information, *distorting* it via metaphor and imagination to help us understand it, to relate to it emotionally, to plan for the future ('What if? ...'). This is the next step young children apply to understand the world: causality – what things in the world is it possible to influence and what can be predicted? An example is: 'Every time I scream, people run into my room: cool!'

Each of these three techniques – deletion, generalisation and distortion – is essential to psychic survival – but they can also be fallible and sometimes very unhelpful.

Let's look at them in greater detail.

Deletion

This is often manifested in vagueness of speech. Such vagueness often hides important material, which is why a good coach will often leap in and challenge it. Here are some examples:

"Vagueness of speech often hides important material, which is why a good coach will often leap in and challenge it."

- **Missing information** – Client: 'It won't work!' To which the coach can reply: 'What, specifically, won't work?' Although this may seem very basic, the client will often answer with something like 'Good question, why did I say that?' Often deletion hides something that is so deep that the client doesn't even know why they said it.

- **Missing or vague subject** – The subject of a sentence is often a great place for people to delete potentially helpful information. Classic examples are: 'They say it's impossible' and 'People say it's wrong to do this'.

- These can be challenged with: 'Who are "they"?' and 'Which people?'

- Another way of hiding information is using the passive voice – saying 'I was pushed' rather than 'X pushed me'. An obvious challenge to 'I was pushed' is 'Who by?' Politicians love this: 'Lessons have been learnt', they tell us endlessly. By whom?

- **Vague verbs** – Verbs can also be vague. A coach can home in on a statement such as 'I was made to do it' for being passive (see above),but also for being vague. How, exactly, were you made to do it?

- **Fuzzy comparisons** – Another form of deletion/vagueness is when a comparison is made – with nothing. The classic example is the old advertising slogan: Wizzo washes whiter. Than what? More subtly, people delete the standards by which they are making a judgement and say things such as 'I was rubbish'. Compared with whom? A club tennis player does themselves no favours comparing themselves with Roger Federer, but people still do this, setting themselves unrealistic standards and then belittling themselves when they don't match up to them. What unrealistic standards does your client have?

- **Unsupported judgements** – These hidden unrealistic comparisons are often preceded with words like 'obviously' and 'clearly'. These are a real give-away! Obvious to whom? Why is it obvious? What is 'obvious' to one person is often not obvious to another, or even 'obviously' untrue! Imagine Richard Dawkins and the Pope sitting down and telling each other what is 'obvious' to them …

Generalisations

As I've pointed out, we need to generalise in order to make sense of the world. If we assumed there were no patterns to events, we would soon go mad. But this tool can be dangerous, as we can make false or hidden links.

The classic version of generalisation is 'All xs are y', but such generalisations normally remain hidden in conversation. More commonly, we see:

- **No exception** – 'Things always go wrong for me'. 'Everyone hates me' (and so on). These can be challenged: 'Always?', 'Everyone?'

- **No possibility** – 'I can't speak in public' is a common one. This can be challenged in a number of ways: 'What would happen if you did?', 'What stops you?', 'Who says you can't?'

- **Moral or psychological imperative** – 'I mustn't become like my father.' The same questions can be asked of these utterances as can be asked of the 'can't' statement above. 'Shoulds' and 'oughts' fall into this category. Challenge them! It's important to understand that in so doing you are not trying to get the client to abandon their values but are questioning moral codes to see whether the client really believes in them, congruently, right now, or whether they are a relic from their (often distant) past. It is not appropriate for a coach to disagree with a client's moral view, but we are there to invite our clients to take a fresh look at these things and to provide a safe space for the client to play with the idea and see whether they want to continue to hold it, drop it or refine it in some way.

Distortion

This is a bit of a catch-all category for ways in which we process information that are unhelpful but that don't fit into the above two categories.

Jumping to conclusions

People often say things like 'He hasn't called. That means he doesn't really like me.'

This may or may not be a valid conclusion. Usually it isn't. Faced with a comment like this, a coach will ask the client to consider other interpretations of the fact that he hasn't called. The coach may also ask the client whether there have been other times in their life when someone hasn't called but that hasn't meant that the person doesn't like them. Or they may turn things round, inviting the client to take what in NLP is called 'second position' and imagine they are the non-caller:

> Does every time you don't call someone mean you don't like them?

Assumption of passivity

The concept of cause and effect is essential to our making sense of the physical world. The classic model is billiard balls: ball A hits ball B, which is determined by physical laws to move at speed x in direction y, which makes it hit ball C, which is determined (and so on ...). However, living creatures, and especially human beings, are not like this: we contain our own causal energy. We make things happen. ('Man was created in order that there might be beginnings', as the mediaeval Christian philosopher St Augustine put it.)

People with depression seem to lose contact with this understanding. They see themselves as either helpless or omnipotent (or flip rather oddly between the two). This can be seen in comments like:

'She makes me angry ...' and 'I made him bored ...'.

The passivity implicit in these statements can be challenged by presenting an alternative view – that people choose to get angry or bored.

Part of NLP coaching is playing the role of a philosopher and explaining the beliefs implicit in the NLP presuppositions. Behind Presupposition 7, 'it is easier to change yourself than others', lies the belief that people ultimately choose how they behave after a given response. Explaining these types of principle to a client is an important function of a coach.

Hidden assumption

Any given sentence is actually built on a huge mountain of presuppositions. Most of these are obvious, so we don't question them. If I say 'Good morning' to the postman, I assume the postman speaks English, that we are referring to our current situation (it isn't morning in Australia), that he will understand the point of the greeting and not start a long philosophical discussion about the nature of 'good' – and so on.

However, presuppositions can be smuggled into statements and have a very detrimental effect. The classic example is the salesperson's *assumptive close*:

Would you like to buy this now or later?

Which, of course, assumes we want to buy. The statement

It is well known that you can't trust young people

assumes young people are inherently untrustworthy.

A coaching session is a great place to dig for presuppositions and examine them.

Turning verbs into nouns

'Nouns', if you've forgotten school English lessons, are 'thing words' such as cat, lorry, Tuesday, London. Verbs are actions, 'doing words', such as act, hit, love, carry.

The turning of the former into the latter is a great curse of management-speak, where instead of asking someone to fill in a form you ask them to undergo a form-filling process. But it's also common in everyday speech. Nouns are convenient buckets into which can be emptied lots of actions. The problem is that this hides subtlety and, more important, cuts off choices: nouns sound solid and unalterable. For example:

Client: My relationship isn't working.

Coach: So, you are currently having trouble relating to each other. What could you do differently?

Here, the noun 'relationship' is converted into the verb 'relate', which is easier for the client to change.

Mind-reading

This is another way we distort reality – by trying to second-guess what other people are thinking. As a kind of party game this is quite fun – and NLP has a number of techniques to make you better at this game. But in real life, mind-reading (or, rather, failed attempts to mind-read) are usually disastrous.

> I can tell by the way she looks at me that she does not like me.

This is a particular problem in close relationships. People some-times say that their partner 'can read their mind' – often with a kind of pride: we are so close that we have this kind of telepathy … But actually, this kind of thinking is a disaster waiting to happen, as one day the partner doesn't read the speaker's mind correctly and is greeted with an aggrieved comment along the lines of 'You should have known what I wanted.'

Coaches need to point out if a client is mind-reading or expecting to be mind-read, and teach them alternative strategies, such as stating what you want or asking the other person what they want.

The Meta Model provides a clear and unambiguous typology of potentially unhelpful ways of thinking (called *violations* in the jargon), and a set of questions and observations to help the client recognise and challenge them.

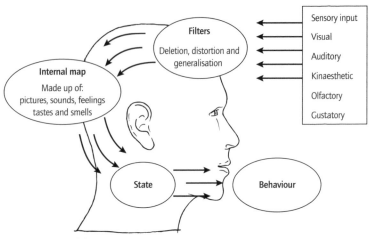

The Meta Model

"Coaches need to point out if a client is mind-reading or expecting to be mind-read, and teach them alternative strategies, such as stating what you want or asking the other person what they want."

Example

Let me illustrate the model at work with an example from a coaching session:

Client: You can't trust people to get things done. [*Notice how this sentence includes various violations. The possible interventions are: 'Which people?' or 'How do you know you can't trust people?' or 'What things specifically can't you trust people to do?'*]

Coach: Which people can't you trust?

Client: Harry.

Coach: What specifically can't you trust Harry to do?

Client: Every time I ask him do something, he messes it up.
          [*Possible interventions here are 'Every time?' or 'Ask him
          to do what specifically?' or 'How specifically does he mess it
          up?'*]

Coach: Every time?

Client: OK, not every time.

Coach: Then when specifically?

Client: The last time I asked him to get a job done.

Coach: How specifically did you ask him to do a job?'

Client: [*Pause*] Well, I suppose I could have given him clearer
          instructions with a deadline.

Coach: What is your learning from all of this?

Client: I better get more organised as a manager, otherwise I
          will become overwhelmed with work.

You will notice how the Meta Model provides a precise methodology, rather than just the usual coaching advice to 'ask powerful questions'.

Because of its power, it is important that a coach uses this material tactfully: after a while these questions can become irritating, and it is important for a coach to calibrate when a client has had enough of this approach and move to a different tack. You can always return to it later in the session if an obvious violation occurs.

The client will soon get the hang of it. Once they start to notice their patterns, it can be enough for the coach to raise an eyebrow when a client says 'I must do *x*', and the client will twig and say, 'That's silly, I mean I choose to do *x*, I want to do it ...'

I have drawn up a table of Meta Model violations. I list the technical NLP name alongside the more useful one – but if you are not formally studying NLP, don't worry about these.

Deletions

Technical name in NLP	Which actually means ...	Classic expression	Challenge
Simple deletion	Missing information	(Depends on context)	'Tell me more ...' 'How, specifically ...?'
Unspecified referential index	Missing or vague subject	'People ...' 'They ...' Use of passive voice	'Which people?' 'Who are "they"?' Rephrase in active voice
Unspecified verb	Vague verb	(Depends on context)	'Tell me more ...' 'How, specifically ...?'
Comparison	Fuzzy comparisons Comparison is empty ... or inappropriate ... or unsupported	'Wizzo washes whiter' 'I'm not as rich as Gates' 'X is happier than me'	'Whiter than what?' 'Is that a fair comparison?' 'How do you know?'
Lost performative	Unsupported judgements	'Obviously ...'	'Who says?' 'Where's the evidence?' 'By whose standards?'

Generalisations

Technical name in NLP	Which actually means …	Classic expression	Challenge
Universals	No exception	'Always …'	'Always? Every time?'
		'Never …'	'Never, ever?'
		'Everybody …'	'Everybody in the world?'
Modal operators of possibility	No possibility	'I can't …' 'It's impossible to …'	'What stops you?' 'Supposing you did …?'
Modal operators of necessity	Moral or psychological imperative	'Should, must, ought …'	'Who says?' 'Supposing you did …?'

Distortions

Technical name in NLP	Which actually means ...	Classic expression	Challenge
Complex equivalence	Jumping to conclusions	'He ignored me, so it's over'	'Does every time you ignore someone mean that your relationship with them is over?' Find some alternative explanations for event
Cause and effect	Assumption of passivity	'You make me angry' 'I make her depressed'	'How exactly?' We all have choice
Presupposition	Hidden assumption	'Do you want to buy now or later?'	Point out assumption Reframe in bigger context
Nominalisation	Turing verbs ('doing' words) into nouns (things)	'Our relationship ...'	Turn the 'thing' back into chosen acts and responses
Mind-reading	Mind-reading	'You should have known what I wanted'	'How should I have known?'

6

SUBSEQUENT SESSIONS AND HOW TO SHAPE THEM

"Coaching is a safe and confidential place where clients can discuss things with themselves."

Ann Baldwin, executive coach

Many subsequent sessions will take a form roughly along these lines:

1 A brief re-entry into 'coaching mode'

2 Some re-contracting

3 NLP processes or other interventions

4 Winding down at the end.

In this chapter I shall look at each of these in turn, and then conclude with some observations about your final session with a client.

Re-entry and re-contracting

The coaching space is a special one, remember, and needs to be re-entered every time. This does not have to be via some elaborate ritual: I just wait till the client is seated, do a little matching and mirroring, look them in the eye, and say:

> So, good to see you again. How's it going?

I focus on rapport, keeping aware of matching body movements until I sense the client is at ease. This can be immediate or may take time, depending on the natural chemistry with the client.

"The coaching space is a special one and needs to be re-entered every time."

I let the client talk a bit about this and that, if they want to. Some clients want to get straight down to business. Great. Others will talk for too long, either because the social interaction of coaching is alien to them or because they want to delay the start. You need to create rapport, but you will be doing the client a disservice if you let them talk for 15 minutes about their recent holiday. Give them three or four minutes and then interrupt. Any professional service provider would do this: a solicitor, accountant, architect, builder ...

What can happen is that the client comes in full of emotion about some new aspect of their life that hasn't surfaced in previous sessions. In this event, the coach needs to ensure that the new issue doesn't get ignored, which would be to 'discount' the client, but at the same time to ensure that the previously agreed list of Areas of Primary Focus doesn't get ditched. So the new issue needs to be noted, by saying something like:

> There's clearly important stuff here. Do you want to do some work on this today?

An enthusiastic 'Yes!' will probably be the answer. Follow this up with:

> Great, we will definitely do that. It is generally useful to start with a list of topics you would like to cover in the session, so what else do you want to work on today?

This ensures that the new issue is on the list of today's topics but has not supplanted it.

Note that if the client has been set some homework, you can suggest that it is one of the topics.

Ideally you want to have agreed on about three topics. A good question to ask when you have such a list is:

> How will you know you've got value out of today?

What you have done here is re-contracting, creating a new contract especially for this session. At this point, show the client the list and ask:

> Which one of these do you want to work on first?

Finding and using the right NLP process

Once a topic is chosen and the client is talking about it, I will be on the look-out for an NLP process that will really help the client with this. I have a mental list of these processes, and my favourite ones are detailed in the next section of this book.

When I get a strong feeling that a process is right for this client at this time, I have to contract with the client to use it:

> There's a process I know that has been very helpful to other clients of mine in a similar situation. Would you like to have a go at it?

Ninety-nine times out of 100 the client will say yes. If they don't, just leave it – the agenda belongs to the client, remember. And in these cases, often the client's curiosity about processes will have been stirred up anyway, and they will ask to have a go in a later session.

Note that it is not necessary for the client to know anything about NLP to use it in coaching: they do not even have to be told it is an NLP process – calling it a 'coaching process' is fine. If clients are curious about NLP and ask what it is, I tell them it is a field of psychology.

Note, too, that some processes are stranger and more demanding than others. If a client is new to NLP, begin with some of the basic processes. And even clients experienced in NLP will need to trust you before embarking with you on a journey like rescripting (see Chapter 14).

Interventions

Sometimes, however, either no process leaps to mind or the client is not ready. Then a more traditional coaching approach is needed. I have already talked about that basics of this: the need for empathic listening combined with keeping half an eye on process (physical and language-pattern signals), the maintenance of rapport, pacing and leading the client to 'learning' states where necessary.

During this phase, you will still be making occasional interventions – not as big as suggesting an NLP process, but still often important. These usually take the form of questions. How do you know which question to ask when? The answer is that your intuition will tell you. The best analogy I can come up with here is musical improvisation. Improvisers don't learn long solos, but they do learn 'licks', short musical phrases. They build up a repertoire of these; then, when improvising, their intuition tells them a particular one will sound good at a particular moment, so they play it. And then, as their mastery improves even further, they surprise themselves by creating something entirely new. (If this analogy is a bit fearsome, remember that we are all highly experienced as conversationalists: it is much easier to reach this level in coaching than starting an instrument from scratch.)

The box below contains a list of classic coaching questions you will want to have in your repertoire.

Your basic repertoire

- What do you want to have happen?
- What would that do for you?
- What could go wrong?
- How would you know when you've got it?

- What's the first step?
- What stops you?
- Can you think of anyone who has done this?
- Knowing that, what could you do differently?
- Put yourself five years in the future: looking back to today, what would you like to have done differently?
- How do you know, specifically, that …
- What benefits do you get out the current situation?
- I notice … How does that seem to you?
- I'm curious …
- I'm wondering …
- What about x [= *another issue*] – is that significant, too, in this context?
- Is there another way of doing this?
- On a scale of 1 to 10, where does this lie?
- What else do you think?
- What else do you feel?
- What is important to you about this?
- I sense there is something a bit stuck here – is this true?
- [*More generally*] I sense *x* – is this true?
- If you were a fly on the wall, watching this situation as a detached observer and not knowing the background, what would you think?
- Can you think of an exception to this? [*To a generalisation*]
- How does *x* specifically mean *y*? [*Challenging mind-reading*]
- Do you genuinely belief that to be the case?
- If you put yourself in their shoes, how would they think/feel about this?

When you start coaching, the question-selection process often involves conscious thought, but with practice you acquire *unconscious competence* and you can just do it. You learn to trust your skill and that the right intervention will 'appear'.

This is where the rapport material can be so powerful: you connect with a client, match their movements and attempt to enter their world without judgement or even wanting to work out what is going on – and often you find that a feeling of some kind is arising within yourself. You can then share this with the client – and what is said can often be truly transformative.

An example of this: I was with a client working through a long goal process, when I suddenly had a strong feeling that he didn't really want this goal at all. Yet he had said that he wanted it badly. I said, 'I have a sense of something, may I share it with you?' The client said yes, so I carried on: 'I just sense you don't really want to do this.' The client looked amazed and said, 'You're right, I really don't want to do it – thank you so much!'

Keeping things going

Over the long course of a number of sessions, it's important to keep the level of listening consistently high, even when the client is going over stuff you've heard before, and it's a hot summer afternoon when it would be nice to out walking in the park and …

"It's important to keep the level of listening consistently high, even when the client is going over stuff you've heard before."

In reality, we all drift off a bit from time to time – the key is to catch yourself doing this, and then not beat yourself up for it but just get back into rapport.

Good coaching sessions tend to have a natural ebb and flow to them. Most of the time, the client leads while the coach listens, watches and learns. Usually at some point the client either hits some kind of inner resistance or just runs out of steam, at which point the coach has to take the reins and get things moving again. If the coach senses resistance, asking the client directly if 'something has come up' usually starts dealing with whatever lurks behind it. If the problem is simply that a train of thought has reached a natural end, the coach needs to find a new area to work with.

You can do this by:

- Suggesting a new topic
- Suggesting a new 'spin' on the old topic – a new interpretation or, going the other way, looking at an aspect of it in greater detail (in other words 'chunking up' or 'chunking down')
- Pacing and leading the client to a more energetic state with your own gestures
- Suggesting coaching at a new level: maybe working on an NLP process or a piece of mentoring. Remember to re-contract for these.

The power of story

Handing out advice directly to clients is not in the coaching spirit – and it doesn't work! As Oscar Wilde said: 'The best thing to do with good advice is to pass it on; it is never of any use to oneself.'

Instead, story can be a powerful but indirect way of suggesting a new course of action to someone. Introduce it with something like:

> May I tell you about something that happened, which may be useful to your situation?

Then tell a story, about a person who was doing one thing but changed.

An example: I was doing life coaching with a client, who had worked so hard on his career that he hadn't had a relationship for a long time. I felt this was what he needed, but I didn't want to say 'Why don't you put in some effort to get a girlfriend?' So I told him a story about another singleton who I had met socially, and who I had asked if a 'fairy godmother' would give him the girl of his dreams but in return he would have to resign from his job, would he do it? The client said he thought this story was rather silly and went back to talking about his work. Two weeks later he phoned me up to say that he had been thinking about that story, and he was going to cut his workload and go to a dating agency.

Wrapping up

I talked about wrapping up the first session in Chapter 2. Most of the techniques used there are needed in subsequent sessions, too. As a reminder, these techniques were:

- The summary
- Homework (if appropriate)
- The closing question
- Attending to post-session comments.

At some point in your wrapping up – after the summary is a good place – refer back to the contract made at the start of the session, when you asked 'How will you know you've got value out of today?', by asking:

> You said that you would know you had got value out of today if … [*whatever their answer to that question was*]. Has that happened for you?

The final session

It may be only six sessions, but coach and client can travel a long way in that time. Finally, however, the journey has to end – or rather this part of the journey has to end. With good coaching, the client goes off into their future armed with what they need, without regrets or yearning for more coaching.

The end is natural on some coaching journeys: the client has worked through the issues they came with and now has a clear set of goals. In other cases, issues might have arisen in the coaching that leave the client with new perspectives on which they need time to reflect.

I generally encourage clients to take a break at the end of the sixth session and let the coaching sink in. If they want more coaching, I suggest they contact me in a couple of weeks and arrange another package, with a new contract. On the other hand if a client simply wants to extend the coaching by an extra session or two, I am happy to do so. One mustn't be rigid about this; the six-session process is only a guide after all.

> **"I generally encourage clients to take a break at the end of the sixth session and let the coaching sink in. If they want more coaching, I suggest they contact me in a couple of weeks."**

The last session is often a great place to use a really powerful NLP process such as the Hero's Journey (see Chapter 12) or Rescripting (see Chapter 14). The client is used to the coaching environment, and has built up their trust in your skills.

Clients often leave really difficult material to the last session. They suddenly realise that this is their last chance to work on the stuff that they know is really troubling them. If they can re-contract to do more coaching, this is fine, but sometimes this is not possible – for example, if the coaching is being paid for by an employer, and the client does not have the resources to become a personal client. As these cases are fortunately rare, when they happen I find it best to offer the client a free session.

That way, I get the work done to my satisfaction and the client gets the full benefit. (I prefer free to cut-price, as that way I keep my 'price point'.)

Less dramatically, closure needs to be brought about by drawing together all the strands that have emerged during the sessions. This means sitting down and looking at the agreed areas of primary focus, one by one, and seeing how goals have been met. It also means looking at any other issues that have arisen.

It also means looking to the future. In NLP we call this *future pacing*, imagining how the 'new you' is going to react to situations in the future. The client can outline their plans for the future.

The sessions should end on a high: a lot has been achieved, and this should be celebrated in some way. The client may need a little gentle leading towards this:

> In the last session it is worth spending a little time reflecting on what you have achieved. Often life can become a bit of a treadmill, running after one goal and as soon as we have got it, running after the next. It is very useful to slow down sometimes and actually focus on the benefits you got on achieving that goal. So, what have been the good things you got out of achieving *x*, *y* and *z*?

And now the sessions are over ...

Having kept a professional distance from the client during the coaching, it's best to keep it that way now the coaching has ended. This preserves the coaching relationship and enables the client to contact you again, should they require your services.

What's more important is that the coaching lasts. The great hypnotherapist Milton Erickson entitled his book *My Voice Will Go With You*: his hope was literally that at times of stress, his clients would hear his voice delivering its positive message. All coaches can have this effect on their clients.

The best outcome from coaching is to find clients becoming their own NLP coach. They may have your voice with them, or they may simply start approaching their issues as interesting puzzles that need to be resolved rather than as negative, stressful and inescapable states.

Subsequent sessions and how to shape them

- Re-entering 'coaching mode'
- Re-contracting
- Finding the right NLP process
- Interventions
- Keeping things going
- The power of story
- Wrapping up
- The final session.

The processes: helping your clients with …

Specific issues and powerful NLP techniques to help clients deal with them

I have designed the next chapters in terms of processes that are increasingly challenging and can roughly be put into the following four groups:

1 Chapter 7 is the classic coaching process for helping your clients to define and meet goals. Chapters 8 and 9 focus on enhancing their performance and dealing with conflicts they may be facing.

2 Chapter 10 contains processes that help clients to resolve troubling past events and to overcome negative states and even some ailments.

3 Chapters 11 and 12 focus on leadership and creativity work.

4 Chapters 13 and 14 deal with helping clients resolve conflicting beliefs and with coaching at the level of Identity. Chapter 15 briefly covers hypnosis.

In the last chapter in this section, I talk about mastering NLP coaching: taking the skills outlined in this book to even higher levels.

Although some clients may want to get stuck into the deep stuff straight away, I find it is best to follow a gentler sequence. Start with the Well Formed Outcome in Chapter 7 and follow it quite closely. Next time start the same way, but allow the process to go a little off-piste: if the client is concerned with a forthcoming stressful event or a problematic relationship, use the Circle of Excellence or the Meta Mirror. This gives the client a chance to become more familiar with the NLP approach to coaching, without going off the deep end. If I do this, in subsequent sessions, I feel able to use any of the processes when relevant.

7

SETTING CLEAR GOALS

"People do not like to think. If one thinks, one must reach conclusions. Conclusions are not always pleasant."
Helen Keller

"Peace is a daily, a weekly, a monthly process, gradually changing opinions, slowly eroding old barriers, quietly building new structures."
John F. Kennedy

The first NLP process I shall look at is called the Well-Formed Outcome. It introduces the client to NLP in a gentle way, and focuses attention on goals and the future, which is the main aim of coaching. I use it in the first session wherever possible.

The process takes the client through set stages. As such, it is not a piece of 'pure' coaching, where the client is totally in charge, and so it is best to contract with the client to do this piece of work before you start. The stages are:

1 Setting the goal

2 Stating it positively

3 'Chunking up' – identifying what is important

4 Making the goal sensory-specific

5 Making the goal self-started and self-maintained

6 Setting a timescale

7 Establishing the context(s)

8   Maintaining the positive by-products of the current situation

9   Checking for hidden consequences or 'ecology' (an NLP term I
will explain in this section).

Setting the goal and stating it positively

The great coaching question 'So, what do you want?' gets the
ball rolling. NLP ensures that the ball keeps rolling and ends up
in the goal.

Clients, especially those with 'away from' metaprogrammes,
often state a goal negatively: 'I want x to stop' or 'I don't want
x to happen'.

The problem is that this focuses the unconscious mind on what
is not desired. If you say 'stopping eating', the unconscious
mind just picks up the 'eating' bit. Instead, encourage the client
to rephrase the goal as a positive opposite of the x you don't
want. So, if the original goal is 'I don't want to be scared', then
say, 'And if you weren't scared, what would you be?' The client
may then say, 'I want to be confident'.

If the client still refuses to state the goal positively, don't fight
with them over this. In these uncommon cases, a positive goal
should emerge in the next part of the process.

Chunking up – identifying what is important

Albert Einstein said, 'You cannot solve a problem with the same
level of thinking that created it': taking the simple opposite of a
negative keeps the same level of thinking. So, once a positive goal
has been selected, ask the client: 'Why is that important to you?'

Iterate this process. For example, if the client replies to the
above that it would enable them to speak with integrity, ask why
that is important (and so on).

This step has a number of functions.

First, it can strengthen the motivation to pursue the goal.

Second, it can bring out previously unnoticed clashes at a higher level. For example, someone who wants to buy a second home may find that, at a higher level, what they want from it is tranquillity. But if in order to buy that home they take on a burden of debt that will actually lessen the tranquillity in their life, they may wish to reconsider their goal.

Third, chunking up may redefine the goal. If the person in the example above wants tranquillity, can they find an alternative way of finding it, for example by renting a holiday cottage in Cornwall for a couple of months in the summer and seeing how that works?

Fourth, if a client was stuck in a negative frame of mind in the previous step, this will almost always lead them to something positive.

If the client still seems stuck with 'away from' outcomes, try an alternative question: 'What would that do for you?'

Making the goal sensory-specific

Clients need to have explicit ways of knowing when the result has been achieved. Ask: 'What, specifically, will you see, hear and feel when you have achieved this goal?'

If you can, include a metric – the more specific the better. But don't just use a figure: for monetary goals, visualise the amount as a wad of cash or a bank statement with the number written on it.

Now, spend some time encouraging the client to imagine they have the goal in the present. This is called the 'as if' frame in NLP. Guide the client through a visualisation of having the goal right now, so they can get a visceral feeling of what success looks, sounds, feels and even tastes and smells like. This will provide an unconscious 'star' towards which the client can navigate.

Making the goal self-started and self-maintained

Goals need to be self-initiated and self-maintained. The client is responsible!

The key here is to break down the journey to the goal into practical chunks, and then get those into a sequential order:

> What is the first step?

> And the next one ...?

The client needs to think through each step in turn. How will they take these steps? What resources will they need to do so, and do they have these resources? If not, what can they do to acquire them? Consider also the environment in which they take these steps. Is it supportive of the journey? If not, what can they change? Ask: 'What do you need to do to keep it going?'

Setting a timescale

> When will the goal actually happen?

Goals that are not timed tend to lose momentum. The client needs to state a time by which they have achieved their goal, and ideally some milestones along the route.

Esatablishing the context

King Midas's big problem was that he didn't set a context for his wish. If he'd wished that everything he touched turned to gold *between the hours of 6 p.m. and 7 p.m. on Monday*, his story would have been very different.

The coach then asks in what contexts the client wishes the goal to apply, and what not:

> When, where and with whom do you want it?

> When, where and with whom do you not want it?

Maintaining the positive by-products of the current situation

Many unwanted situations bring positive side-effects or 'by-products'. Being addicted to tobacco may be a source of stress, but smokers also benefit from some positive by-products, such as being part of an exclusive club or having a ritual that allows them to regularly take five minutes out of work. So ask: 'What good things do you get out of the present situation that could change if you got this goal?'

It is also worth going up the Logical Levels: many people have beliefs that preserving the status quo will avoid huge amounts of stress, but this can be challenged using the Meta Model. Also people can identify with existing behaviour: many smokers recall coming of age and state that they knew they were a 'real man'/'real woman' when they first started smoking. Generally it is sufficient to ask the client, 'Do you need to keep smoking to be a real man/real woman?' The client will usually laugh and say, 'Of course not, and yet strangely I needed to say that.' (Much of the job of a coach is to witness what the client has to say: once they have said it out loud to another human being, that is often enough, in itself, to resolve the issue.)

Positive by-products can be sorted into 'must haves' and 'would likes'. The 'must haves' need to be replaced by something else, or the client may sabotage the goal-achieving process. The 'would likes' can be negotiated away, usually by comparing the small amount of benefit they bring with the huge benefit that the goal will offer.

Ecology

In NLP, *ecology* means 'fitting in with the bigger system'. In the case of a goal, does it fit with the overall scheme of the client's life?

Finally, ask these three questions:

- 'There will be costs, both financial and other, going for this goal. Are the costs worth it to you?'
- 'This goal will take time, time you could spend on other things. Is the time spent on this goal worth it to you?'
- 'Lastly, in terms of your sense of self, do you see yourself as someone who can achieve this goal?'

The process may get stuck at any point. The positive by-products section often reveals consequences that the client is unwilling to take, or at least take at this point in their life. Similarly, the three questions above can often bring things to a halt. This is, of course, a good thing, as the client now has a better view of themselves. It can open up the proverbial can of worms, which will provide material to discuss and, I hope, resolve in future coaching sessions.

Example

Here is an example of this process in action. The client is a youngish man, currently in employment, keen to set up on his own but nervous about doing so:

Coach: The first thing I'm going to do is ask you 'What do you want?'

Client: To be self-employed.

Coach: OK, lovely. Now what I'd like you to do is imagine that you are self-employed already. You've left whatever employment you're in and you're now self-employed and you have some kind of income stream coming in. Just have a sense of being self-employed right now. How does that feel?

Client: Yes, good.

Coach: Sometimes it's just simply kind of nice to imagine you actually have the goal right now. Having that goal of being self-employed right now, just allow yourself to notice what would that allow you to experience – in other words, why is that important to you?

Client: It would give me more freedom.

Coach: More freedom, lovely. So have a sense of having more freedom right now – what would that do for you that is even more important?

Client: I suppose give me more choices.

Coach: More choices. Just pretend you had that right now. You've got all the choices you want right now, and with all those choices what does that allow you to experience that's even deeper and even more important?

Client: I suppose being able to go in any direction or any direction that I want to go in.
[*Now it's time to move on to making the goal sensory-specific*]

Coach: Great. Let's go back to that original goal. What would you see if you were self-employed right now? Give me some sensory evidence of what your life would look like, what it would sound like, what it would feel like.

Client: I suppose it feels like there's more movement, more energy.

Coach: More energy, more movement ... [*The client gestures to a certain spot when he says this; the coach does the same, to emphasise the point, and then carries on with building a mental representation of the goal, using all rep systems*] So imagine you're self-employed; where would you work? Would you work from your home, would you rent an office, would you be with someone else? What would it actually look like, the place where you do your thing?

Client: Quite comfortable, quite welcoming, quite warm.

Coach: Welcoming and warm ... [*These are rather general kinaesthetic terms, indicating the client's preferred system, so the coach gets more specific*] Would it be on the first floor, the ground floor?

Client: Ground floor.

Coach: Do you have any idea of the location?

Client: On the high street.

Coach: What else do you see? Do you see any clients, customers, that kind of thing?

Client: Yes. People walking past, people coming into the shop.

Coach: What do you hear?

Client: Not a lot.

Coach: No, I sense that. Also what about feelings? Tell me a little bit about what you notice internally, now, having that goal of being self-employed right now. [*Note the use of slightly hypnotic language (now ... right now ...). The coach is helping the client associate with the goal as deeply as possible, which in turn will help them achieve it. This is the thinking behind the book* The Secret]

Client: I suppose my breathing is wider.

Coach: Your breathing's wider?

Client: Yes, I get a sensation just around here.

Coach: [*Lets client repeat gesture and hold it for a while*] Imagine going there; you've got it and it's all worked out wonderfully and it's all fine. Just notice the feelings, the pictures, the sounds just for a few moments, even some smells and tastes. Now will you be able to remember that?

Client: Yes.

[Pause before starting the next part of the process]

Coach: What would you say is the first step in getting to this place?

Client: Just working out, I suppose, how much it would cost and the practicalities.

Coach: So, working out how much it would cost and the practicalities. Give me an idea, I don't know, what would be the very first step, the first thing you'd do?

Client: Just go round and have a look, look around and see what's available and what's possible.

Coach: Premises-wise?

Client: Yes.

[They go through a process of planning out the actions, step by step, which I shall leave out of this transcript]

Coach: What would you do to maintain the momentum on this project so you would keep going with it week in, week out?

Client: I suppose keep feeling how I feel now, trying to focus on how I feel now about actually going for it.

Coach: OK, and how would you do that?

Client: Try and visualise what it looks like and what it feels like, how it feels.

Coach: How would you remember to do that?

Client: Think about what we're doing now and being here and focusing on it.

[At this point, the coach could push the client into being more specific – making a note to do that visualisation and set some goals every Wednesday at 8 a.m. In this case, the coach did not do this, sensing the client was very congruent

about remembering to do this and would do so without such a 'ritual']

Coach: Let's look at timing a bit. When do you want to start moving to being self-employed?

Client: This year.

Coach: And how much time do you think you'll devote to it?

Client: I'm not sure. Half a day a week?

Coach: Half a day a week. Do you know when you'd do it? Any particular day or just whenever?

Client: Fridays.

Coach: And with whom do you want this outcome?

Client: Just myself.

Coach: What about the contexts in which you don't want the outcome?

Client: I don't understand what you mean.

Coach: This feeling, this buzz of having your own business. You may not want it when you're out with a mate. You might not want it when you're having dinner. You might not want it when you're doing other work. This is about allowing you to not have to worry all the time, about not having to focus on the goal when you're doing other activities.

Client: OK, so when I'm working, leisure time at home.

Coach: Good. That might seem a slightly obvious point, but it's useful because it also gives you some boundaries of when you can do it and when you can't do it, so that you don't feel guilty. [*The coach pauses, then moves on to the 'positive by-products' section*] We have the saying in coaching: 'If you wanted it that badly you'd have it already'. What we mean by that is that there's something good that you're getting out of your existing life that you would possibly have to give up to become self-employed. So I want to write down all the good things you currently get out of being employed – things that you think you might have to sacrifice if you were to become self-employed.

[*The coach takes notes at this point, for use when running over these points later*]

Client: Regular income ... Paid holidays.

Coach: Anything else?

Client: A team that I get on well with.

Coach: Let's just unpack that one a little bit. What are the good things you get out of being in a team that you get on well with? What are the benefits to you of that team or being part of that team?

Client: Working together.

Coach: What does working together do for you?

Client: I think I enjoy working along with other people.

Coach: So there's a sense of enjoyment, you enjoy working along with other people. [*Note the exact mirroring of the client's language by the coach*] Anything else?

Client: Well, that's the big one. I like the company.

Coach: OK, we'll press on. What else do you get out of being employed?

Client: Courses, education.

Coach: I'll pry a little more, if I may. With the education, do you also get some element of support or mentoring or development or something positive like that?

Client: Coaching.

Coach: Coaching. What are the benefits you receive from that?

Client: Benefit is ... you develop and move forward.

Coach: Okay, develop and move forward. [*Client nods. A brief silence follows. The coach has thought of something, and this has taken their attention away from the client, who in turn has run out of things to say*] There's also another thing that sometimes is worth asking. Having your own business means that you'll be the boss. Is that something that is of benefit or is that irrelevant to you? What's the view on that in terms of your own sense of self?

Client: It's not really that relevant, I think.

[*The coach has gone out on a limb, sensing the client was not mentioning a key issue. But the client seems congruent about not being fussed about the boss issue, so the coach moves on, getting the session back on track*]

Coach: In sales training they talk about 'must have' versus 'would like' benefits: I must have this; I would like that. So let's go through each one of the benefits from your current situation, and tell me whether it's something you must have or you would like. So, regular income: is that something you must have or would like?

Client: Must have.

Coach: Paid holidays?

Client: I think it's got to be a must have as well.

Coach: A team that you get on with and work well with?

Client: Would like.

Coach: Enjoy working along with other people?

Client: I like that.

Coach: Must have or would like?

Client: It's a must have.

Coach: Education?

Client: Would like.

Coach: Development?

Client: Must have.

Coach: OK, so you're now self-employed and regular income – how do the two sit together?

Client: Being self-employed has to provide a regular income for you to be able to keep yourself and sustain yourself.

Coach: So you'd need to have a regular income to sustain yourself. But when you start a business you're not going to get a salary. How do you reconcile those two?

Client: So you need some additional money to start with to tide you over.

Coach: So some savings. What kind of savings? Do you have an idea of what level of savings would be enough for you to be able to start?

[*The coach is drifting into being a bit of an adviser here, but the client is not troubled by this*]

Client: Yes.

Coach: Now, paid holidays.

Client: You need to be able to take some time away to be able to continue going or stop burning out.

Coach: Does that block you from being self-employed in some way or not?

Client: A little.

Coach: So that's something again that we could explore if we had more time but it's an interesting point, isn't it? Is there any way round it that you could think of?

Client: Just structure your time so that the times where you see your clients or whatever you're doing, you could take some time off but you're not going to lose money.

Coach: So you could try and structure your holidays around when work isn't available or something so you wouldn't lose money, OK?

Client: Yeah.

Coach: Enjoy working along with other people – how would you resolve that with being self-employed?

Client: Find other colleagues, people interested in what I do or doing the same types of things in their work.

Coach: So it's networking, finding other people who do the things you do and that sort of thing ...

Client: Yes.

Coach: Lastly, development. How will you maintain your own personal growth and development through the process of starting your own business?

Client: Again, seek help of other people doing the same things, I suppose. Mentorship.

Coach: So finding a mentor, mentorship, meeting other people, find out how they do it. Find some strategy to achieve that . . .

Client: I can do that.

Coach: OK, great. Now I want to do a quick thing called an ecology check. When we talk about ecology in NLP we don't just mean the environment, we mean any type of system and how it all works together. If something changes in the system, then sometimes that throws the whole system on its head.
I want to ask you three questions and I want you to just give me yes or no answers coming from the gut. You don't need to think about them, just yes or no. There's going to be costs involved with this goal. Is it worth it to you?

Client: Yes.

Coach: You really meant that, I can see.

Client: Yes.

Coach: It'll also take some time to deliver this outcome, time that you could be doing something else. Is the time worth it to you?

Client: Yes.
[*This appears congruent, too. Lastly, the coach checks whether the client is happy with the goal at the level of identity*]

Coach: Also in terms of your sense of self, do you see yourself as somebody who's self-employed?

Client: Yes.

Coach: OK, lovely. Well done.

Tips on the Well-Formed Outcome

Although it is worth following this process step by step the first few times you do it, it can become rather wooden doing so after a while. The order of the questions, although useful, can change to slot in with the flow of the coaching session. If an organised client presents a goal that is clearly defined and well structured, it is unnecessary to repeat questions they have already answered. The key to mastery of this process is to have a list of the nine items you can mentally tick and elegantly cover in the flow of a session.

"If an organised client presents a goal that is clearly defined and well structured, it is unnecessary to repeat questions they have already answered."

Well-Formed Outcome coaching script

1 Set the goal – 'So, what do you want?'

2 Ensure it is stated positively.

3 'Chunk up' – 'Why is that important to you?'

4 Make the goal sensory-specific – 'What, specifically, will you see, hear and feel when you have achieved this goal?'

5 Make the goal self-started and self-maintained – 'What is the first step? And the next one? What do you need to do to keep it going?'

6 Set a timescale – 'When will the goal actually happen?'

7 Establish the context(s) – 'When, where and with whom do you want it? When, where and with whom do you not want it?'

8 Maintain the positive by-products of the current situation – 'What good things do you get out of the present situation that could change if you got this goal?'

9 Ecology check:

'There will be costs, both financial and other, going for this goal. Are the costs worth it to you?'

'This goal will take time – time you could spend on other things. Is the time spent on this goal worth it to you?'

'Lastly, in terms of your sense of self, do you see yourself as someone who can achieve this goal?'

8

PREPARING FOR IMPORTANT EVENTS

"He that wrestles with us strengthens our nerves and sharpens our skill. Our antagonist is our helper."
Edmund Burke, philosopher

Coaches are often confronted with clients who are worried about a forthcoming event, for example giving a speech at a major conference or having to break up with a partner. Traditional coaching will use a conversational approach to help clients prepare for such events, walking them through the event and discussing ways in which they could deal with issues and emotions that arise. This can be very helpful, but sometimes people need a bit more – which is what this chapter is all about.

The Circle of Excellence is an NLP process that combines various positive memories (and their associated states) together into one state, which can then be brought about by a simple trigger. The coach can then guide a person through a rehearsal of the event, using the trigger to access the new state when they need it.

"The Circle of Excellence combines various positive memories into one state, which can then be brought about by a simple trigger."

The process involves a technique called anchoring, which I shall now describe.

Anchoring

An anchor is a trigger that instantly creates a new state.

In daily life we have many anchors. Typical anchors are feeling good (or bad) when you hear someone's voice on the phone. Perhaps a particular song takes you back to a specific memory. Places, people, clothes, sounds, smells, touches, words and tones of voice can all act as anchors.

Anchoring is essentially about creating (or dismantling) anchors in ourselves or in other people. To create an anchor in someone, we get them into the desired state and then apply the anchor, the stimulus that we wish them to use in the future to bring about that state.

It's exactly what Pavlov did with his dogs:

In 1902, psychologist Ivan Pavlov ran his famous conditioning experiments with dogs He rang a bell whenever food was brought to the creatures. Then he started ringing the bell without bringing food, and he found that the dogs still salivated (a sign of getting ready to eat) at the sound of the bell.

He then experimented with more dogs, ringing the bell at different times: shortly before the food arrived, exactly as the food arrived, and shortly after the food arrived. Then he rang the bell without food again and found that in all cases the dogs started to salivate at the sound alone; but the dogs for whom the bell had rung at exactly the same time as the food arrived salivated the most. In other words, they had made the strongest association between the sound and the food.

The skill of anchoring lies in knowing the right moment to apply the stimulus – the moment when the client is most strongly associated with, most deeply into, the state (the equivalent of Pavlov ringing his bell exactly as the food arrived).

You can ask clients to tell you when they have reached this state – 'Give me a nod when you're there ...' but the catch is that many clients will lose the intensity of the state once they enter into judging how intense the state is. There's no substitute for calibrating the client, watching them and spotting from their physical signals when this state of maximum intensity has been reached. Look for signs of peak energy or a sudden change of expression.

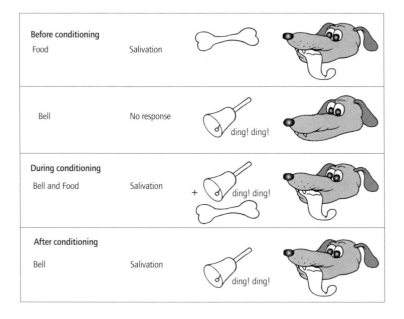

Anchoring is often done with a touch – kinaesthetic anchoring – but in the Circle of Excellence (and in many other NLP exercises) the anchoring is *spatial*: the anchor is a particular place. Our brains are amazingly precise about this: different parts of a room can act as anchors for totally different states, provided that we mark out clear spaces and stick to them.

Anchoring techniques

Though there are many ways to anchor, they all follow a similar process: *elicitation* (bringing about) of a state, followed by anchoring, associating that state with a stimulus. This exercise takes you through that process step by step:

1 The client decides on a state of mind that they wish to anchor.

2 The coach then discusses and agrees with the client what the anchor will be. A good kinaesthetic anchor is a quick, reasonably firm touch with one finger on a knee or arm.

3 The process proper begins. Coach: 'Let me know when you have thought of a specific time when you had that state.'

4 'Go back to that time and see what you see, hear what you hear, feel what you feel, and fully relive that now.'

5 The coach watches the client carefully, to identify when the experience of the desired state reaches a peak ...

6 ... Then the anchor is applied.

7 *Break state*: this is a common technique in many NLP processes. The client has to change their mood/mindset. It can be a simple thing: stretching is good, as is shaking your body, taking a few deep breaths or concentrating attention on a previously unnoticed object in the room.

8 The coach reapplies the anchor on the client and asks if it works.

9 Repeat a few times to strengthen the anchor.

The Circle of Excellence

Our thoughts and feelings affect whether we operate from a centre of strength or from a vacuum of weakness. By first building and then spatially anchoring the first type of state, we can create a tool we can use to ensure that we operate from our best, especially at times of stress. Here's what happens:

1 The client selects an upcoming event where they are nervous about having to perform in some way.

2 The client imagines a circle on the floor that is big enough for them to step into.

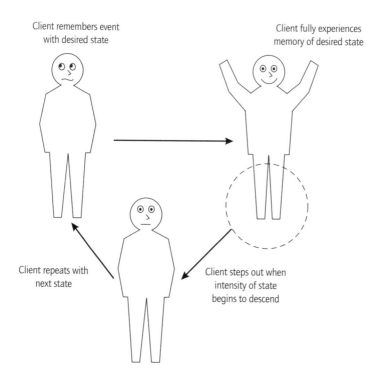

Client remembers event with desired state

Client fully experiences memory of desired state

Client repeats with next state

Client steps out when intensity of state begins to descend

3 The client identifies a smallish number of qualities or resources they will require in the upcoming stressful situation.

4 They prioritise these resources.

5 They take the most important resource and identify a time when they were in possession of it.

6 Once they have done this, but before they are fully associated with the memory (in other words, they are aware of it but not reliving it), they step into the circle.

7 Once in the circle, they associate as fully as possible with the memory. What do they see? What do they hear? What do they say to themselves? What kind of body posture do they assume? What gestures do they make?

8 When the intensity of the memory begins to lessen, they step out of the circle again and break state.

9 Repeat stages 5–8 for each resource they selected at stage 3.

10 Outside the circle, they create a metaphor for the state of having all the resources on their list.

11 They step into the circle again. Coach: 'Bring all of these qualities together. Notice how they combine into something new and powerful.'

12 The client spends time imagining they have all these things and enjoying this imaginary experience. When they are ready, they step out of the circle.

13 Break state, then test. The coach asks, 'Was there anything missing?' If the client congruently says 'No', move on; otherwise recycle through steps 5–12 again and incorporate any additional qualities.

Later ...

14 Now it's time to use the exercise. Tell the client you are going to take them through the lead-up to the upcoming challenging event and that you are going to ask them exactly when they want to be able to access the resources. (In other words, do they want them when they get up that morning, when they arrive at the building where the event will happen, or the moment before it begins?)

15 Do this. When you have established when the client wants the resources, take them to that point and get them to create and step into the circle. For example, if the client says 'Just before I walk through that door', the coach can say 'OK, stand up and imagine you are walking through the building – just before you open that door, the circle is there in front of you. Actually, stand up and do this now, and notice as you stand in the circle how changes take place.' [*Calibrate the client, they may need some time here, when they are ready ...*] 'Then you slowly reach for the door handle ...' The client can imagine the circle on the ground in front of them, step into the circle and fully recall and associate with the state they felt in stage 12. This should fill them with the resources they needed in step 3, and

they can go out on stage or into the boss's office (or wherever) armed with these things, and in a positive state of mind.

Example

This example doesn't follow the outline above word for word. But I feel it captures the salient points well and shows the process in action. The client is a woman concerned about an upcoming meeting with her boss.

Coach: Do you have any idea of where this meeting will take place?

Client: In her office.

Coach: Fine. Let's be more precise. When exactly are you going to need extra resources?

Client: I'd like them when I'm sat opposite her and we're about to talk.

Coach: Fine. Lay out a circle on your chair, then. What resources would you like when you sit in that chair?

Client: Resources?

Coach: I mean things like feeling relaxed or confident.

Client: Relaxed. I'd like that. And sure.

Coach: Relaxed and sure ... Any others?

Client: I've heard various things about this person that she's a bit of a backstabber. A bit devious. I don't want to get caught up in all that sort of stuff. Actually, I don't want to have these prejudices about her.

Coach: So what would you like instead?

Client: Openness.

Coach: Right. Relaxed, sure, openness. Any others?

Client: I would probably be a bit more decided about how I deal with how conversations go and how I feel – all that sort of stuff.

Coach: What quality would you call that?

Client: Prepared, maybe.

Coach: So relaxed, sure, openness, prepared. Any others?

Client: I'm partly wanting to say the word 'professional' because my way of coming across isn't professional, it's a bit more relaxed.

Coach: Professional. [*Client nods. Brief silence*] Is that enough?

Client: Yes, that's enough.

Coach: I'm going to put the resources in order of significance, so let's prioritise. If you could only have one of these, which would it be?

Client: Relaxed.

Coach: If you had a choice of the remaining four, which would it be?

Client: Probably sure.

Coach: We're now going to go through these, which is a sort of ritual in a way to make a Circle of Excellence or, in this case, a chair of excellence. Let's start with relaxed. Think of an instance when you had 'relaxed', any event, and I don't have to know what it is. [*Notices client's expression*] You've got it. [*Note that the coach doesn't encourage the client to 'associate' with the instance, just to be aware of it. The full, intense re-experiencing of the event will follow, once the client is in the circle*] OK. Now sit in that chair. [*Client does so*] Go fully into that memory RIGHT NOW. [*Pause*] Allow yourself to see what you see, hear what you hear and feel what you feel. [*Pause*] FULLY RELIVE THAT SENSE of relaxed RIGHT NOW.

[*The coach emphasises the capitalised words. When the client looks like she has 'been to' that memory and moved on ...*] Now, leave the chair ... [*The coach then does this for each of the other resources that the client mentioned. Note that the coach uses the exact words that the client gave – the coach will say 'Fully relive that sense of sure' next time (and so on).*]

Now it is time to combine all the resources and anchor them all. Remember, the client is now standing outside the circle] Do you have some kind of metaphor for how you felt in there?

Client: Lovely. Free.

Coach: A metaphor – a picture perhaps?

Client: Walking in mountains. Fresh air, lovely views …

Coach: Walking in mountains. Fresh air, lovely views. Great. Now, just to check – is there something missing?

Client: No, not really.

Coach: Great. Now we come to the crunch. You said that you were going to be sitting opposite your new boss. What's she called?

Client: Karen.

Coach: So you're coming into Karen's office. And there's the chair. Create the circle there, and now enter it. Just imagine what it's like.
[*Client steps into the circle again*]

Client: It feels fine. Thank you very much.

Tips on anchoring in the above process

In the part of the process when the client identifies relevant memories (step 5, or in the example 'Remember a time when you had "relaxed"…'), the coach needs to manage the client's state so they can identify the time *without* going fully into (= reliving) that memory. The client needs to enter the memory to some degree so they can judge whether it will give them the resource they need, but if they then carry on and fully associate into it, this reduces the power of the anchoring once they are in the circle. You need to stop them once they have thought of a memory and judged it to be a useful one; but if you jump in too quickly, you'll put them off and they may lose the memory and have trouble getting it back. The skill, therefore, is to watch the client closely and, when you think they have found the memory and just thought 'Yes, this has what I need', ask them something like 'Have you found a memory yet?'

Different clients access and assess memories at different speeds: you have to learn what pace they go at. Their first memory-search will usually be some kind of guide: if they find the first one quickly, the others will probably be found quickly too.

"Different clients access and assess memories at different speeds."

Note that some clients don't want to be guided through the memory-finding process, but they can then fall into the trap of fully associating with the memory while still outside the circle. Say to them: 'You may find it more powerful if you allow me to guide you through the process ...' and they will usually agree.

Tips on visualisation

The majority of people can imagine pictures in their mind's eye. A small percentage (myself included) find this hard: I do not see pictures when I close my eyes. For clients who share this issue, NLP has a solution: pretend you can see things. (This is a common NLP intervention. If a client says they can't do something, an NLP coach will often say 'Pretend you can'. This often shifts the block.)

All people process visually; it is simply that some people do not hallucinate images when they do so – to prove this, consider that we are able to recall a person's face when we meet them, which means we must be comparing the face we see 'out there' with a face we have stored in our memory. By pretending to see, you create the same effect as actually seeing something you are pretending to see. In the modelling and inner rehearsal section in Chapter 19, I suggest a method to help build the internal visualising 'muscle' by combining it with our innate sense of space known as proprioception.

The Circle of Excellence

The client:

1 Selects a future event where they want to perform at their best

2 Creates an imaginary circle on the floor

3 Selects resources that they will need to make a success of the future event

4 Anchors those resources, one by one, into the circle

5 Rehearses by stepping into the circle and pretending the event is happening now.

9

DEALING WITH CHALLENGING RELATIONSHIPS

"If you hate a person, you hate something in them that is a part of yourself. What isn't a part of ourselves doesn't disturb us."

Herman Hesse, writer

In this chapter I shall introduce material that can be used to resolve client issues in all relationships except the most traumatic ones. Once mastered, this material gives the coach both a formal process they can use and, more subtly, a tool that can be used conversationally to consider virtually any situation – a problematic relationship, how a product or service might be received, or simply improving influencing skills.

Perceptual positions

This concept gives us the ability to take multiple perspectives on a situation: from our perspective, from someone else's, and from a perspective where we are not personally involved. This increases our flexibility and allows us to see more deeply into a situation or system. Each perspective (= position) gives new information, and the combination of the different positions leads to what many people define as wisdom (as opposed to cleverness, which is a narrower ability to achieve a goal whatever the consequences for others).

"Each perspective gives new information, and the combination of the different positions leads to what many people define as wisdom."

Looking at the three positions in turn …

First position

This is our own personal perspective: seeing through our eyes, speaking our thoughts, having our identity, beliefs, values, desires (etc.). When speaking from first position, people will talk about themselves in the usual manner, as 'I' and others as 'he', 'she' and 'they'.

To get maximum value from this position, you need to banish 'self-censorship'. Allow yourself to be selfish!

Second position

> Never judge a man till you have walked a mile in his moccasins.
>
> Navaho saying

This is the perspective of another individual (or, sometimes, group). It involves seeing through another's eyes, speaking their thoughts (as you imagine them to be), taking on their logical levels. The best way to take second position is to copy the gestures, posture and language patterns of the person involved. The language you use will again be 'I' (now 'being' them, of course). You and third parties will be 'he', 'she' and 'they'.

If you speak in public, taking second position (with your audience) briefly before you start is a very useful exercise, as it allows you to understand and predict their needs and reactions.

Third position

In third position you are external to the main actors in a scene, as if looking at it from the outside – the position of the fly on the wall, or of the traditional detached novelist who lets you into the thoughts of all their characters.

If you are taking third position to yourself in a conversation with your partner, you will see both yourself and them, and will refer to both parties in the third person ('he' or 'she').

This position is often known as 'meta-position'. (*Meta* is Greek for a higher category.)

Some people find certain perceptual positions easier to take than others. People with strong personalities may find it a challenge to suspend their habitual first-position way of seeing and understanding the world. Other people are uncomfortable with taking first position: the spouse who constantly makes sacrifices for a partner is a classic example of this. Other people are most comfortable in third position, that of the external analyst.

All these positions have their advantages and disadvantages. The habitual taker of first position will probably know what they want but be insensitive to others' needs. The habitual taker of second position will be seen as kind and giving but may also be weak and can become passive-aggressive. The habitual taker of third position may suffer from 'paralysis by analysis', always ready with theories and models but unsure of what they actually want to do with them.

It's useful to deliberately practise consciously assuming the different positions, especially those that you feel least comfortable with. Each one is important: the three positions can be neatly mapped on to Stephen Gilligan's interpretation of Jung's archetypes (natural energies that are the basic building blocks of human existence):

- **Strength** – First position, the ability to assert boundaries and to form a clear view of who you are and what you need and want
- **Softness** – Second position, the ability to connect with others and the capacity to see their viewpoints
- **Playfulness** – Third position, the ability to form an overall view of what is going on, and the creative lighter touch needed to move forward.

In time it gets easier to flip between positions and use the information you gain from so doing to guide your choices.

The Meta Mirror

This exercise is useful for finding new ways forward in difficult relationships. It can also help clients re-examine situations from the past that didn't turn out satisfactorily.

Like the Circle of Excellence, it uses spatial anchoring and associates specific locations with mental states (in this case, the different perceptual positions), though it does so in a less intense way. The process works best in a reasonably large room; that way, you get clearly different 'locations' with which to associate states – so rearrange the furniture and give the client space.

Beforehand …
The coach checks with the client that:

■ He or she has a clear issue with someone with which they want to work

■ He or she has decided upon a specific example of incident that raises that issue, which the client will re-enact.

The coach asks the client to describe where the incident took place. The client then lays a bit of paper on the floor to represent where he or she was situated when this happened (first position) and a second piece of paper to indicate where the other person was situated (second position). The coach then asks the client to lay out a another piece of paper as third position, ideally equidistant from first and second position.

The coach then asks for the name of the other person in this scene. Rather boringly, I will call this other person X and assume that the client is called Y.

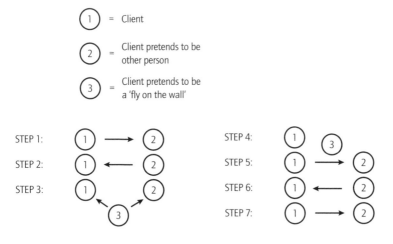

Step 1

The client stands in position 1 as themselves, looking at the other person, whom they imagine to be standing over there in position 2. The coach asks: 'What is the other person's name?'

Once the client has replied (with 'X'), the coach says: 'Looking at X over there, tell me what you think and feel about them.'

Once the client has done this, they are to step off position 1 and 'break state'.

Step 2

The client walks over and stands on position 2, facing position 1. The coach says: 'I would like you to pretend to be X. When you are ready, step into that person and take on their posture and facial expression.'

When the client is fully 'identified' with the other person, the coach says: 'Look at that person, Y, over there, and tell me what you think and feel about them.'

Note, it is important that once the person is fully in second position, the coach talks to them as if they were the other person, in other words calls them X.

Once the client has done this, the coach says: 'OK, stand off that space and break state.'

Step 3

The client walks over and stands in position 3.

(a) The coach says: 'Look at those two people over there. Pretend they are strangers; what do you notice?'

(b) When the client has answered, the coach says: 'What qualities or resources might the person in position 1 need to make this situation improve?' The coach needs a list of three or more qualities, so ask 'Anything else?' if only one or two are forthcoming.

(c) Then ask: 'Taking the first quality you mentioned, can you remember a time when you had that quality, perhaps in an entirely different situation?' (Ideally, the memory should not be of a situation similar to the one the client is working on, but if the client can only come up with a similar memory, work with that. If the client is stuck, it can be useful to point out that the memory can be quite a trivial one.)

(d) When the client says 'Yes' ask them: 'OK, go back to that time. What is it like?' The coach is getting the client to associate with the memory, but in a less intense way than in the Circle of Excellence. The client doesn't have to relive the memory moment by moment, but it is important that they have some 'feel' of it, not just recall it intellectually.

(e) Once that is done, the coach asks questions (c) and (d) again for each of the qualities the client listed. As in the Circle of Excellence: the client is assembling a list of desired resources and of relevant memories, which will then be associated with a physical space.

Step 4

The client does not need to 'break state' this time but simply leaves the third position space and stands outside the system.

The coach says, 'OK, take the qualities you found in position 3 and transfer them over to position 1. You might like to use your hands to do this – any way you want to do this is right.'

Clients normally intuit what this means and make a kind of shoving gesture.

Step 5

The client walks over and stands in position 1 again, as themselves. The coach says, 'OK, take some time to receive those qualities.'

Pause while the client does this.

The coach says, 'Now look at X, over there. Have you changed the way you think or feel about them?'

Step 6

The client walks over and stands in position 2 again (where they become the other person). It's good to remind the client to take on the posture, physiology, facial expression (etc.) of the other person.

The coach says, 'OK, look back at that person in position 1, who now has the new resources. How do they seem now?'

The client replies.

When they are done, the coach pauses for a few moments, and then invites the client to step off the space and break state.

Step 7

The client returns to position 1 as themselves.

The coach asks, 'How is it now?'

Tips

Often the position that is most unfamiliar to people is second. Doing this well is a bit like method acting – in an ideal scenario a client literally 'becomes' the other person, imagining having had their childhood, gender, race and experience. They will use the same gestures, accent and voice tone; they will imagine wearing their clothes and having the same hair and body shape. They truly become the other person, with an attitude of non-judgement and curiosity.

In reality, most people find this difficult to do, unless they have some theatrical experience. They often see it as 'weird' and a childish form of playacting. However, the human brain contains areas – mirror neurons and the fusiform face area – that actually model and mimic other people, so these skills are actually hard-wired into us. Coaxing people to 'do' second position involves a mixture of pointing out these facts, and using a bit of charm, humour and perseverance. Sometimes it is easier to repeat the second position a few times. After a rather half-hearted display I often say, 'I really didn't buy that. Go on – have a proper go; you have nothing to lose and you may find something worth-while . . .'

For people who have trouble entering third position, use a story such as 'imagine you saw two complete strangers in a restaurant . . .'

In third position, it's important for the client to be as objective as possible and not to interpret. 'X is angry' is an interpretation; 'X has a frown' is objective. If the client insists on the former, press them for their evidence.

A good mix of qualities for the client to wish for at step 3b is that of the Gilligan/Jung archetypes: words such as strength, compassion and perspective. Although it is important to use the client's words, if the client suggests, say, power, ruthlessness and willingness to crush, these are all one quality and the coach can pace and lead the client to a wider range.

Example

The client is a woman who has a difficult neighbour. Note: the pieces of paper have already been set out on the floor.

Coach: Now, this person again. What's her name?

Client: Estelle.

Coach: And what happens with her?

Client: She makes me feel dreadful about myself. Her screaming and shouting. She gets on the telephone and has a go at me ...

Coach: Right ... I'd like you to tell me a particular situation with her from the past. It would be better if she was actually present rather than being on the phone.

Client: Well, she came to the house one day. I wouldn't let her in, so we stood outside ...

Coach: Excellent, we're going to relive that. Position 1 is going to be where you were actually standing, so go into that position. Where exactly were you standing?

Client: On the doorstep.

Coach: And she was?

Client: About a yard from me.

Coach: Fine. There she is in front of you and she's shouting and so on, and what I want to know is what comes up in you at this moment?

Client: I'm scared. And I feel like I'm being used.

Coach: Do you have a real sense of those feelings right now?

Client: Oh, yes.

Coach: Good. Now I'm going to ask you to step off the paper, and then jump up and down to try and get rid of that horrible feeling. Shake it away. Has it gone?

Client: Kind of, still there.

Coach: Shake a little more then. That better?

Client: Yes.

Coach: OK. So if you'd go and stand behind 'position 2' and imagine her standing on it as if she was a hologram, how does she dress?

Client: Smart. Shoulder pads, heels, the bloody works.

Coach: So you can imagine that. Now I'm going to ask you to step on to the paper and be her. Ready?

Client: Yes. [*Does so*]

Coach: So, Estelle, get into that posture, the power dressing. Those heels ... Just allow yourself to feel that. So what's happening?

[*Note that the coach is now addressing the client as Estelle, the person with whom she has the issue*]

Client: Part of me won't let her in ...

Coach: Just pretend. Don't judge her; just for a moment suspend the anger and be curious. I wonder what's going on in her head? Just go in and just see if anything unusual comes up – you never know ...

Client: OK ... I'm getting there.

Coach: Good. Yes, that's right ... [*Points to position 1*] Estelle, look at Sheena [*The client's name*] over there. Can you see her? What do you notice?

Client: She's completely different from me and she seems really comfortable in her life. I'm angry, and I'm going to take it out on her.

Coach: Good. Let's move on to position 3, fly on the wall. [*Client does so*] Now you can see these two women; you've never met them in your life but there's obviously certain things going on. Tell me what you see – be as precise as possible.

Client: It's kind of like a tiger and some animal it's after, a goat or something.

Coach: Hmm. That doesn't strike me as very objective. You've never seen these two before, you don't know them from Adam. You're walking down the street in a strange town, and you see these two women. You know nothing about them. There's something happening, there's some kind of interaction between these two women. What do you notice very scientifically, specifically from their facial expressions, from their voice tone, from their gestures? What would you assume is happening in this connection?

Client: One is angry. The other is afraid. She doesn't want to be there ...

[*The coach could press the client to be more specific at this point but doesn't*]

Coach: OK ... Consider this: if there was a quality that the afraid one could have back there in that situation at that doorstep, what quality do you think would have made the interaction easier for her?

Client: Confidence.

Coach: Confidence, great. [*Notes this down*] Others?

Client: Communication. Self-belief possibly. Maybe a little bit of anger actually.

Coach: So something like assertive.

Client: Yes, a bit assertive.

Coach: Does that not map into confidence a bit or is it different?

Client: For me it's different, yes.

Coach: What about something like detachment or in some sense not taking it too seriously?

Client: Yes.

Coach: What would you call that?

Client: Detachment is fine.

Coach: Lastly, a difficult one in this case, but what about a little bit of empathy?

Client: Yes.

Coach: Would that be helpful?

Client: Yes.

[Note – the coach has broken the rules here, suggesting a thought to the client. Welcome to the reality of coaching: this happens from time to time! But note that the client accepts it]

Coach: OK. Now do you remember at time when you had a sense of confidence? It doesn't have to be anything dramatic. Just buying something in a supermarket will do fine.

Client: Yes.

[The coach then goes through the list the client gave, getting the client to produce a memory that goes with each resource. When the list is complete ...]

Coach: So what I want you to do magically is take those qualities that you explored – confidence, communication, self-belief, assertiveness, detachment, empathy – and somehow give them to the 'you' back on position one.

[The coach explains the process. The client then follows it. She steps outside the system. Looking at the third position place, she makes a kind of gathering up gesture, picking up the resources, then mimes throwing them at the first position location]

Client: Whoo! They're gone.

Coach: Great. So now we're going to and step back into the situation but, wait a moment, you have these new qualities! So step back into position one. *[Client does so]* You can accept these things: confidence, communication, self-belief, assertive, detached ...

Client: Confident, communicating, self-belief, assertive. What was the last one?

Coach: Detached.

Client: Oh yes. Detached.

Coach: Take time to take in those five things. Remember the memories, take them in now ... *[Pause]* How does that feel?

Client: Good, yeah.

Coach: Now we've got one more step. Be Estelle again, the high heels, all that stuff. [*Client goes to position 2*] Now Sheena has all those new qualities, how does it feel now?

Client: I can't do what I did.

Coach: Now be yourself again, here, now. [*The client walks over to the first position location*] How did that feel?

Client: I felt completely different. It's not just her making me feel a certain way; it is me making her feel that way as well, so maybe perhaps if I change how I am she might change a bit how she is too.

Dealing with challenging relationships

The client:

1   Selects a specific, unpleasant interaction with the other person.

2   Takes up three mental positions and anchors these to three separate spaces in the room:

- First position is that of themselves

- Second position is that of the other person

- Third position is that of an objective observer of the interaction

3   Experiences the interaction from first and second positions

4   From third position, identifies resources that would be helpful to themselves in first position and then transfers those resources over.

10

HEALING TROUBLESOME MEMORIES

"A memory is what is left when something happens and doesn't completely unhappen."
Edward de Bono, psychologist and writer

One of the main benefits NLP has to offer is to help change habitual negative responses.

Before I learnt NLP I knew that I had some 'choice' on how I responded. However, when I was tired and when I received a certain 'look' or tone of voice, I would find my state had changed automatically and I was upset. After a while I would calm down and feel foolish for yet again entering into this negative state.

What I learnt from NLP is that often our responses are unconscious, so the idea we can completely control our feelings is, for most of humanity, an illusion. I also learnt that these responses are often triggered by the current situation stirring up an old memory, and it was that old pain that I was really reacting to. NLP offers ways of changing the way people 'code' these original experiences. Once I had undergone these recoding processes, I found that in many circumstances I simply stopped getting the negative emotional response – a sort of psychological miracle!

Note that troublesome past experiences can also generate unwanted physical responses: under stress many people develop symptoms such as headaches, rashes and stomach aches. These 'recoding' processes can also change these responses too.

Of course, I still have negative responses, just a lot fewer. In these cases, I can still control how I behave: despite the NLP model and the power of these processes I don't like using 'programming' as an excuse for bad behaviour.

I begin this chapter with an important feature of all NLP coaching, finding out the positive intention of a negative response. Two processes follow: Mapping Across to change how we respond to negative states, and New Light Through Old Windows to overcome negative (note, not traumatic) old memories. At the end of the chapter, I shall consider how this material links with physical health.

Positive intention

Remember NLP proposition 3, 'all behaviour has a positive intention', and the thinking behind it, that the behaviour once served – or still does serve – a useful purpose. The key for the NLP coach is to find out what that purpose is, and to help the client explore new ways of meeting the same end in a more constructive and relevant way.

Here are two examples:

During a recent coaching session, a client was speaking about his plans and long-term goals. I sensed that he had talked about these in a similar way many times before: his voice tone was monotonous and lacked passion. I also noticed that his foot was stamping at certain moments, which gave a rather strange emphasis to his speech. After he had spoken, the following dialogue took place:

Coach: I sense something was coming up in you during that discussion; I noticed you were stamping your feet a bit at times.

Client: [*Ponders for a few moments*] Yes ... It's strange, but there is something blocking me.

Coach: What do you think this blocking feeling is trying to do for you? [*This is the question about positive intention*]

Client: That's odd. I feel it is trying to protect me. I get a sense that it doesn't want me to feel the disappointment and pain of failure.

Coach: What else could you do to protect yourself, to minimise that issue?

Client: I guess all I have to do is start on a smaller scale and treat any mistakes as vital learnings rather than as failure.

Coach: How does that blocking sensation feel now, if you were to start on a smaller scale?

Client: [*Smiles, and speaks emphatically*] Great, there's nothing stopping me now!

This is a very common result of NLP coaching: the client has some unconscious block and, by 'doing a deal' with that block, a huge sense of energy and relief is released.

Here is another example, with someone who complains about being unable to lose weight:

Client: I am really overweight. I just can't lose it. I have tried so many diets.

Coach: What does being overweight do for you?

Client: I ... I don't know. [*Grimaces*] I know this seems crazy, but it makes me feel safe.

Coach: Safe from what?

Client: Safe from being hurt again.

Coach: Hurt by whom?

Client: By men.

Coach: Any man in particular? [*Note the use of the Meta Model here*]

Client: Bill.

Coach: Do you believe all men will treat you like Bill?

Client: No, but I got really hurt.

Coach: What else could you do to protect yourself from being hurt again in the future?

Client: Well, I could make really sure that he was the right one, before committing myself.

Coach: And, if you did that, would it then be OK to lose weight?'

Client: Yeah, I will simply say 'No' unless I am really sure; it would be great to have that lighter feeling again!

In business, people are often hobbled by the 'tall poppy syndrome'. Don't succeed, don't stand out. Behind this can hide a range of different positive intentions: honouring a client's poor background, parents who were disappointed by their career and didn't want their child to feel the same, a need to be one of the lads or one of the girls … Often when this is brought into a client's conscious awareness, new ways of meeting these needs present themselves. For example, the client needing to honour their background can visit their family or old friends, or, if they came from a specific religious tradition, start eating certain foods.

Working on this aspect of behaviour is one of the most important parts of any significant NLP coaching. Often, when I look back on a session that seemed to get stuck, it is because I didn't coach the client through this vital piece of the puzzle.

Mapping Across

This process is a way of transferring resources from a client's repertoire of positive states to a state or states that is or are currently a problem.

It uses spatial anchoring, positive intention and a new NLP concept, that of *submodalities*.

The concept of submodalities takes the idea of rep systems further. Earlier we talked about people storing information visually, auditorially or kinaesthetically. These are *modalities*. Now we go a level deeper, to look at exactly how this storage is done.

When a client recalls a certain memory, do they remember pictures? If so, we can ask all sorts of questions about the picture. Is it moving or static? Is it in colour or black and white? Is it in a frame of some kind? Does it appear right close up to you or in the distance? This enables us to drill down into exactly how the client stores imagery – and later, we can invite the client to tinker with that storage, which in turn can change the way they feel about the image (for example, moving an image from right in someone's face to a long way away can greatly lessen its power).

This concept doesn't just apply to visual images. A list of ways in which we can change the way that images, sounds and feelings are stored is given in Appendix E.

I am going to present this process as a coach script:

1 'Tell me about the problem context.'

2 'Please write on this piece of paper a word that can act as a label for this problem.'

3 'Tell me about a resourceful context, such as a pleasant time with friends or time spent in nature, to act as an alternative. Again, write a label for this on another piece of paper.'

4 'Please put these two pieces of paper on the ground close enough so you can easily step from one to the other.'

5 'Stand on the resourceful piece of paper and tell me what you see, hear and feel.' [*The coach should press the client for details of the submodalities of the seeing, hearing and feeling, not just ask about content, and carefully note the responses*]

6 'OK, step off the paper and break state. Now go and stand on the problem context and tell me what you see, hear and feel.' [*As above, press for details of submodalities and note responses*]

7 'Please step off the paper and let me explain an interesting concept. The problem state wants to communicate something to you. As your unconscious cannot talk to you, it behaves a bit like a child and upsets you to get attention. If you can believe this to be true for the next few minutes, would you

be willing to let your unconscious generate some alternative behaviours and let you know in the course of the next few days or weeks what they are?'

8 'When you identify what it is your unconscious wants you to do differently – and it is always an overall positive thing – will you promise now to act upon it?'

9 'Now step back on to the problem piece of paper and remember the images you experienced there.' [*Tell the client all the submodalities you recorded at Step 6*]

10 'Now put one foot on to the resourceful paper … And notice how each aspect of the [*negative label*] transforms into aspects of the [*positive label*]. [*Describe each submodality change one by one*] That's right.'

11 'Finally, when you are ready, fully move over to the resourceful paper. And now you can fully notice how things can be much better …'

12 'How is it now?

New Light Through Old Windows

This process uses submodalities and a new NLP concept, association and dissociation.

If we are *associated* into an experience, we are involved in it, living it as if we were in the situation, seeing it through our own eyes, re-experiencing the event and caught up in the action. If we are *dissociated*, we experience the event from outside, as if we are watching a fairly dull movie: we can see ourselves on the screen and do not feel a strong emotional involvement with what is going on: we are able to interpret the action in an objective way.

"If we are associated into an experience, we are living it as if we were in the situation. If we are dissociated, we experience the event from outside."

Our capacity to move from one to another allows us to detach ourselves from a once-powerful image and look at it more objectively. It takes the emotional charge out of the situation, and we can then learn from the image. An example: a client had a negative feeling about his ability to play sports. He remembered a time in early childhood when a sports coach said, 'You aren't good enough to play, go sit over there.' By dissociating from this memory and using the process below, the client was able to repair the damage it had on his beliefs by bringing his current adult wisdom to bear on a childhood event. A classic piece of NLP work!

Process

1 Ask the client to think of a troubling (not traumatic) past experience.

2 Ask them to visualise that memory again and ask them to gesture to a point in space where they see it.

3 Calibrate whether they are associated or dissociated with it.

4 Ask them whether they see themselves in the memory. If they do, move to step 5. If they do not, ask them to step back and put themselves in the memory, at the age they were when it happened. Notice whether they appear more dissociated at this point.

5 Ask them to explain the situation to you while watching the movie in a dissociated state. Make sure they stay dissociated and don't get involved in it.

6 Now we are going to invite the client to adjust the visual submodalities of the memory by changing the location of the movie screen to increase the effect of the dissociation.

Ask them to move the screen further away, closer, up, down, left, right, even to view the filming from above like a cameraperson on a boom crane. Continue to do this until they confirm that the new location has helped them become more dissociated from the original memory. Often at this point the client has a sudden realisation.

7 Help them access the learning. 'As you watch this movie from this new angle, and look back on that experience, what do you learn now?' Your language aims to maintain the dissociated state.

8 Make sure they have a clear piece, or pieces, of learning.

9 Test. 'How do you feel about that experience now?' If the learning is complete, the experience will no longer trouble them.

10 If they are still troubled, ask the positive intention question, 'What are the benefits of preserving that memory as it is?' (Some coaching may be required to find alternative behaviours that can honour the positive intention.) You can also run the exercise again and see whether the client finds a new, and more therapeutic, perspective.

11 Apply the new learning elsewhere. 'Take the learning and apply it to other times in the past where it would have been useful.'

12 Ask them to 'whisper in the ear' of that younger version of themselves in the movie, offering any advice or support that would have helped them get through that experience back then.

13 Future pace. 'Take the learning to a time in the future where it will be useful, and imagine using it.' The client can do this from an associated position as well as a dissociated one.

A note on memories

Some clients are nervous about changing or altering their memories, fearing that this will in some way tamper with their identity. But this process is not about changing the memory but how that memory is *experienced and interpreted* by the client. Changing these can be very healing indeed. Here again, we see the impact of positive intention: a client may not engage with a process like this as their positive intention is to preserve their identity. Some coaching of their beliefs around memory will help them.

"Some clients are nervous about changing or altering their memories, fearing that this will in some way tamper with their identity."

Health

I have used the material in this chapter with people who have had certain illnesses, including eczema, asthma, migraines and tinnitus, and who have subsequently had complete remission. In other cases, the material has helped people develop a strategy of how to avoid an attack of certain chronic conditions, such as malaria and lupus, so they pick up the signals early, rest and avoid a full-blown flare-up of the illness.

I do not believe NLP can cure all illnesses, but I do believe that a component of illness can be within people's volition and NLP can provide access to that volition and bring about helpful change.

There is, of course, a negative side to this belief. The more you say 'illness is in the mind', the more you encourage a kind of fundamentalism that tells sick people that the illness is somehow 'all their fault'.

On a practical level, I wait to be approached to use NLP in dealing with illness rather than volunteer it when I hear someone is ill. Partly this is because a person who actively approaches me is more likely to believe that NLP in general (and I in particular) can help, and this belief is going to play an important part in healing – the power of the placebo effect, but also the power of intention, which is stronger when shared by coach and client. (A point about the shaman story I cited earlier is that the patient also had an intention to get better.)

There are two excellent books on this subject: Deepak Chopra's *Quantum Healing* and Ken Wilber's touching *Grace and Grit*, which deals with the death of his wife Treya and the dangers of fundamentalist approaches to health.

Healing troublesome memories

■ **Positive intention** – Finding the positive root cause of unhelpful behaviours.

■ **Mapping Across:**

1 Client takes two pieces of paper, writes the name of a problem state on one and the name of a desired state on the other, and puts them on the ground.

2 Standing on the 'positive' bit of paper, client is encouraged to fully recall a relevant memory.

3 Standing on the 'negative' bit of paper, client is encouraged to fully recall a relevant memory.

4 Client commits to act upon some future information, whenever it is discovered.

5 Client starts on negative bit of paper, recalls all of the memories, and then stands on both bits of paper, transforming negative to positive, ending on the positive bit of paper.

■ New Light Through Old Windows:

1 Client recalls troubling (not traumatic) memory.

2 Client imagines memory as if they could see it on movie screen right now.

3 Client inserts their younger self into the screen if necessary.

4 Coach encourages client to move the screen to different locations, until client feels reduced emotion.

5 Client brings more mature understanding to the situation and learns new lesson.

6 Client 'whispers in the ear' of younger self in the screen and gives them advice and support.

11

BOOSTING CREATIVITY

"Creativity is allowing yourself to make mistakes. Art is knowing which ones to keep."

Scott Adams, creator of 'Dilbert'

The process I shall present in this chapter helps clients unleash the natural creativity that every human being possesses.

The process was created by Robert Dilts. One of Robert's interests is in modelling success, and one of the successful people he modelled was Walt Disney – a highly successful business leader, remember, not just the voice of Mickey Mouse.

When looking at Disney and his methods, Dilts was told by a close associate of the cartoonist/entrepreneur: 'There were actually three different Walts: the *dreamer*, the *realist* and the *critic*. You never knew which one was coming into your meeting.' Essentially, the dreamer was the optimistic creator of new ideas, the critic the sceptical tester of those ideas against reality, and the realist the person who got on with the job of turning those ideas into reality, step by step.

The dreamer, the realist and the critic can also be seen as archetypal characters, each with their own energy. Freudians will spot the similarity with id, ego and superego, and the TA ego states of Child (Dreamer), Adult (Realist) and Parent (Critic) map well on to these archetypes, too.

The process

1 The process starts by creating three separate spaces where the client can associate into the three states of Dreamer, Realist

and Critic, and fourth space, a 'metaposition' from which to take an objective view of what is going on.

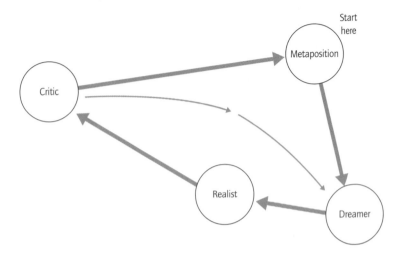

2   Write the words on pieces of paper and put them on the relevant spaces. This is best done quickly, and without the client thinking about what is on the paper and what they are going to think about when they stand on it: the spaces need to start the exercise 'clean' and free of any associations.

3   Starting with the Dreamer space, the client is asked to stand behind the piece of paper and recall a time when anything seemed possible. As with the Circle of Excellence, the coach needs to manage the client's state so they can identify such a time without associating fully with the memory. Once the client has done this, ask them to stand on the Dreamer space.

4   Now the client can really get into the memory. Say: 'Go fully into that memory RIGHT NOW, allow yourself to see what you see, hear what you hear and feel what you feel – FULLY RELIVE that sense of possibility RIGHT NOW.' The coach will gesture for the client to focus straight ahead or up to right.

5   The client is asked to do the same thing with the Realist space. They are to recall a time when they were practical, hands-on, getting stuff done. (Note that the physiology of a realist is

usually looking directly ahead, sometimes marking out specific actions with gestures.)

6   The client is asked to do the same thing with the Critic space. They are to recall a time when they were aware of the faults in something and pointed them out, clearly and assertively. (The physiology here is often head to one side, eyes looking down, often with the hand supporting the chin in the classic 'thinker' pose.) It is generally advisable to locate this space a fair distance from the Dreamer and Realist as some people find the Critic a bit of a put-down.

The last three stages have anchored states to locations.

7   The client is asked to step on to the metaposition space and to discuss the outcome they want to achieve.

8   The client goes to the Dreamer position. They are asked to see themselves accomplishing the goal. The coach may ask questions to encourage creativity and imagination, for example suggesting that the client imagines they are the director and writer of a movie, free to create whatever pictures they want. Time in the Dreamer place gives the client a chance to be liberated from the constraints of current reality and just to explore.

9   The client is asked to step on to the Realist position and consider what realistic steps they can take to accomplish the dream. The coach will ask questions to focus the client on realities, about specific actions, deadlines and the sequence of steps needed to achieve the goal.

10 The client is then asked to step on to the Critic position and criticise the plan devised by the Realist. The role of the Critic is to criticise the *plan* but not to criticise the *dream*. The coach will ask the client to focus on what might go wrong and to anticipate any threats to the project.

11 The coach asks: 'Can you dream up some solutions to the problems you have discovered in the Critic space?' The client

steps back to the Dreamer position and dreams up alternatives that answer the Critic's concerns.

12 Cycle through steps 8–11 several times. The key role of the coach as this happens is to ensure that the client is on the right place. For example, if the client says 'It will never work ...' when standing on Dreamer, the coach asks the client to continue in the same vein but to move to the Critic space, where such thoughts are appropriate. After a while, clients get the hang of this and start naturally going and standing on the right position for the voice that is having its say.

13 When the client feels that cycling through the steps is no longer adding new ideas, they can put the project aside and continue walking through the Dreamer, Realist and Critic positions, this time thinking about anything: daydreaming or thinking of something that he or she is already good at and enjoys. This starts the unconscious mind processing the information and can add different perspectives and resources to the process.

14 Check. Does the client have a plan that each role can agree with congruently? If yes, conclude the process. If not, revisit any objections.

Clients can fear the critic position. The critic position tends to combine a protective 'street smart' side with a 'scary' parental voice – sometimes called the 'Spoiler' – that can make an individual clam up. The client needs to learn to differentiate between these two, listen carefully to the former and suspend the latter, dealing with it later as a separate therapeutic exercise.

The Spoiler is often a mixture of self-doubt and reminders of disempowering memories of parents. Have a go at a process such as the Meta Mirror, New Light Through Old Windows or Parts Integration (to follow) to resolve these issues.

The positive critic is often highly creative, and their input can make all the difference between a fine-sounding plan that won't actually work and a plan that is really robust and effective. The client needs to learn to respect and like it.

"The positive critic is often highly creative, and their input can make all the difference between a fine-sounding plan that won't actually work and a plan that is really robust and effective."

We all tend to have our favourite roles in this process. Two of the points of doing this exercise are to realise which our favourite roles are and to understand that other people will have a different preference (and that as such they are not 'opposed' to us but actually are bringing something very useful to the party).

When I was managing my business, I saw myself as a realist. But I had somebody working for me who was a dreamer: after initially writing the guy off as a bit of a fantasist, I learnt to value his input.

Example

The client is a female middle manager keen to raise her game at work.

Coach: Let's start first with the Dreamer. Can you walk over to that space, please? [*The client does so*]
Now I sometimes think of a dreamer state as one when you made big plans in your life. Do you remember a time like that?

Client: Yes.

Coach: So I'd like you to just step on to the space. You might like to close your eyes if you want, and just remember that time when you had that sense of being a dreamer, that anything was possible and you were making all sorts of plans. Go fully into that memory, right now. Allow yourself to see what you see, hear what you hear and feel what you feel – fully relive that sense of possibility, right now …' [*The coach calibrates that the client is fully associated with the memory*] Great. You have that sense. You can step off the piece of paper. The next one we're going to do is Realist. [*The client heads over there*] You don't need to pick a huge event in your life. I mean 'realist' could simply be planning a shopping list. Just when you set out, what do I need, when am I going to need them by – it's that kind of energy, that quality, that I'm looking for. So can you think of a time when you were a realist?

Client: Yes, when I do my business plan.

Coach: Brilliant. Are you doing it in Excel or on paper? How do you do it?

Client: Excel.

Coach: So then just remember the situation. Just reaccess that now and when you've got it you can step off … [*The client does this. Afterwards, she does the same with the Critic space, then steps back into the centre of the room*] So, tell me your goal.

Client: One of my goals is to get ten deals done bringing in up to £2 million.

Coach: Excellent, OK. So ten deals bringing in £2 million. When would you like to get that done?

Client: Well, realistically by the end of next year.

Coach: 31st December?

Client: Yes.

Coach: OK. Let's go back to the Dreamer space. [*The client does so*] I'm going to invite you to explore that with me. So I'm going to ask you some questions. The first question is what do you want?

Client: I want a very successful department.

Coach: If you had a very successful department, what would that do for you?

Client: Make me feel confident about myself and ensure a promotion and hopefully a pay rise.

Coach: If you think about having that pay rise and that great sense of confidence right now, what would that make possible?

Client: Clients would perceive me to be better, and therefore it would be easier to win business.

Coach: Great. Let's move forward. So pretend it's now 31st December, next year, and I'm Roly [*her boss*] and I come up to you and say, 'Well done, it wasn't £2 million, it was £3 million! Great work!' You've got that right now? Good. Now what does that make possible?

Client: It makes it possible to get more promotion. Even to start thinking about a place on the board … If you get that level, you just grow in confidence, you grow in knowledge, you grow in expertise, and you build from there really.

Coach: And where would you see yourself, say, ten years down the line? Just allow yourself to dream.

Client: Well, on the board. Why not?

Coach: Great. On the board. So step off that space and sort of shake that off. You can guess where we're going now, the Realist. What's the first step?

Client: I've forgotten what the first step was.

Coach: £2 million worth of business by the end of next year. So now we're going to be very practical and reaccess the Realist state. Now you're standing here with your business plan in Excel. What's the first step from here to there?

Client: I've got a new client who says he can introduce me to other people in his network. My first step is to get to know him better.

Coach: OK, lovely, and when will you do that?

Client: We're meeting next Tuesday, actually ...

Coach: And what's next? [*They then spend a while discussing other steps she could take*] Great, thanks. That all seems nice and realistic. So now we have to be the Critic. You remember being critical, not necessarily suspicious but critical. Whenever you're ready you can step on and just remember being the critic means sometimes being the spoiler. So this is a key point: we don't criticise a dream, we criticise the plan. People are allowed to dream. So looking at your plan, just take a look at some of the points you came up with – what could go wrong?

Client: Well, he mightn't like me as much as I hope. [*Coach nods*] And this network may turn out to be non-existent. God, I've heard that stuff about 'my network of people' so many times ...

Coach: OK. Now go back on to Dreamer again when you're ready. [*The client does this*] So let's look at these objections. The guy mightn't like you ...

Client: Well, that happens. But I'll make sure I look nice – it all helps, you know. And I'll make sure there aren't any mistakes with booking and so on. And I'll do that Circle of Excellence thingy we did the other day in the taxi on the way over there so I'm in the right frame of mind.

Coach: And what about the network?

Client: Well, again, if that's the case, it's the case. But I can worry about that if it happens. I shall go in taking the guy at his word – that's more positive, isn't it? Actually, that will help when we first meet. Gets things going in the right mood. [*The client nods, falls silent, looks happy*]

Coach: All right. Well, I think you can step off that. The last place to visit briefly I think would be the Realist. So whenever you're ready ... [*The client returns to the*

Realist space] So moving forward, what are you going to do differently to take into account some of those things you just said there?

Client: Be more positive. Trusting, but not naive. It's a balance thing, isn't it?

[*They discuss a few more 'to dos', then finally the client looks up, smiles and steps off the paper*]

Coach: So how did you find that?

Client: Good. I think I am a realist at heart. The dreaming part is harder. I can't just come up with a really big dreamy picture … But the critic made me think actually that the problems that I think are there probably aren't as big as they might seem sometimes, so that was really helpful.

NLP Creativity Process

- Based on the actual practice of Walt Disney

- Three mindsets anchored to spatial locations:

    - Dreamer – comes up with new ideas

    - Realist – works out how to put them into practice and creates a plan

    - Critic – on the look-out for flaws in the plan

- Note difference between 'critic' (looks for problems but in a helpful way) and 'spoiler'.

DISCOVERING A CALLING

"He who has a why to live can bear almost any how."
Friedrich Nietzsche, philosopher

Here is a process to help clients identify their calling or mission in life – a process for the coach as awakener. For some clients, this helps them gain personal confidence and self-belief; for others, it helps build a shared mission as leaders in certain endeavours. In many cases the outcome is the client's realisation that their striving has already delivered the goods in their life and that they can accept and enjoy their life as it is.

The Hero's Journey

This process was designed by Robert Dilts, based on the work of anthropologist and philosopher Joseph Campbell. Campbell analysed traditional stories from around the world and found that they followed a similar pattern. The research was published in *The Hero With a Thousand Faces* in 1949, and the book has been used by Hollywood screenwriters ever since as a template for movie plots.

Campbell broke down the archetypal story into sections. There are a number of these, some of them rather arcane. In a simplified version, there are seven:

- Hearing the calling
- Accepting the calling
- Crossing the threshold
- Confusion to clarity
- Gathering assistance

■ The battle

■ The return home.

I shall begin by looking at this model of how stories work, and then take you through the process based on it.

The calling

The story begins with a hero (the term is used to describe protagonists of either sex). The hero is usually in an unsatisfactory condition but not doing anything about it.

Then they receive a *calling* to do something about this. Initially, they usually *refuse the calling*, as it involves too much risk or simply inconvenient change. However, things get worse, and some event changes the hero's mind, so they *accept the calling* after all.

Crossing the threshold

Having decided to act, the hero has to leave their existing world and cross a *threshold* into a new one. The way across this may be barred by *guardians* who try and stop the hero getting across: the hero has to find a way past them.

Confusion to clarity

Once in the new world, the hero will experience *confusion*. However, a view of how things are becomes clear: the source of the trouble in the world they have left is a *demon*, and the demon is here in the new world and needs to be fought.

Gathering assistance – mentors and helpers

The demon is scary and looks all-powerful: the hero needs all the help they can get. So they seek help. This help can often be a wise old man or woman with magical powers – a *mentor*. Other *helpers* are gathered or attach themselves to the voyager, too.

The battle

The demon is finally confronted. To make the story exciting, the good guys usually fare badly at first. Then there is a turning point. Often, at this moment the hero undergoes a *transformation*; they learn something of immense value or undergo some personal change that enables them to turn things around and win.

Often, once this transformation is effected, the demon changes, too. It either turns into something feeble, or it loses its malevolence and turns into a helper for the hero.

The return home

The hero has to bring from the new world some kind of magic elixir that will right the wrongs of the world they left behind. In some stories, the hero will be reluctant to return; in others, they have to fight battles to get back. For whatever reason, the return home can be quite slow (in Hollywood, this is rarely the case, as movies require an action climax and then a quick end, but in traditional myth – and in coaching – the return can be lengthy and incident-filled).

In the end, the hero returns with the elixir to the old world, delivers it, and gets on with life again, transformed but still 'of the world'.

It is worth briefly explaining the model above to the client, telling them about the key concepts – calling, threshold, mentor, demon (etc.) – so when you use these unusual terms the client is familiar with them. (They may also find a trip to the cinema much more interesting afterwards!) I often draw this out on a piece of paper.

The Hero's Journey script

Note that the process does not follow Campbell's model precisely but rather uses the key concepts. The issue for clients is often that of accepting a calling. This process is a way of acting out, in the 'as if' frame, a mini-drama: 'Supposing you did accept the calling and go on the journey – what would you do and what would you end up with?'

As a result, the 'elixir' in Campbell's model is referred to as the 'calling' in the NLP process. Dilts means that at this point, the calling, heard back at the start of the story, has now been achieved (in this imagined mini-drama).

Part 1 – characterising the journey

- **The calling** – 'What are you being called to do or become?'

- **The demon** – 'Is there something on the route to doing or becoming this that frightens you, something scary that will need to be dealt with at some point?'

- **The threshold** – 'The journey to accomplishing a calling means leaving where you are now, your "comfort zone", and going to new places. Tell me about the entry point, or threshold, to this new world.'

- 'What *resources* do you need to accomplish your calling?'

- 'Who are, or who will be, your *mentors* for those resources? You may want to pick people you know, or famous people or even characters from books or films. You may wish to choose mentors who embody a certain quality, such as strength, compassion or a sense of humour.'

Part 2 – setting out the timeline

Present Accept *calling* Threshold Mentors Demon Calling Future ▶

1 'Please lay out a timeline showing where the future and past are.'

2 'Point to where on this line you want to have the threshold, the demon and the point where you have fulfilled your calling.' It can help to put pieces of paper on the floor for each of these.

3 'Please also show where your mentors would stand, beside (not on) the line.' As in step 2, use pieces of paper as markers if that helps.

Part 3 – going on the journey

4 'Have you accepted the calling?' If the client doesn't say 'Yes' immediately, it is worth finding out whether there is an obvious reason why, though don't spend too long on this as the process itself will identify any blocks.

5 'Let's start just beyond the present, where you have accepted the calling.' I don't usually bother with a piece of paper for this point, but it's somewhere between the present and the threshold. Note that clients sometimes think that the point where they accept the calling and the threshold are the same. But the two points are different. Accepting the calling is an internal thing. It's that moment when you've been pondering a course of action for a while and you wake up one morning and say to yourself 'Yes, I'm going to do it!' After this, you probably do a number of actions: crossing the threshold is the one that changes the world you are in irrevocably. For example, if someone has accepted the call to go and do voluntary work in Africa, crossing the threshold is when they get on a plane and head off to the unfamiliar new world in which they have agreed to serve.

6 'Where is the threshold and how is it stopping you?'

7 The coach can role-play pushing past the threshold with the client, by having the client physically push at them and by resisting. The coach asks the client to notice where in their body they feel the resistance and to notice the thoughts

come into their mind – these may often throw interesting and unexpected light on the client's situation.

8   Once they are past the threshold … 'Before you face the demon, please step in to each of the mentors and pretend to be them.' (Using the language of the Meta Mirror in Chapter 9, the client assumes second position in this step.) The client walks up the timeline to the point opposite where they have placed their first mentor – for the purposes of this example, let's say it's Winston Churchill. 'Go and stand over there where Winston is standing.' The client then steps off the timeline and on to the spot associated with the mentor, and turns to face the line again. 'What advice do you have for him/her, Mr Churchill?' (The coach gestures to where the client was previously standing.) The client, as mentor, offers advice.

9   'Now go back to the timeline, face the mentor and receive that advice.'

10   Repeat steps 8 and 9 for each mentor.

11   'Please now walk straight to the calling as if you had already resolved everything.' (Note that this is a departure from Campbell's model: it misses out the battle. This might look as if you are missing the big moment, and certainly won't be copied in Hollywood, but it works better in coaching. The point is that the demon often transforms without even being confronted if the process is done this way.)

12   'Now turn back and look at the journey. Ask yourself if there are any other resources that you need to push past the threshold and to face the demon.' The client then sends a message back to themselves in the present. (The content of the message is up to the client, but it is often encouragement or a piece of advice.)

13   The client returns to the present – walking beside the timeline but not treading on any of the mentors' spaces – and receives the message. They will usually want to pause a while to take it in.

14 'Now go to the threshold, push past with your new physical strategy. Be aware of your mentors and notice what has happened to the demon.'

15 You may wish to step on to the space occupied by the demon and become it. What is it telling you? It may even become a mentor.'

16 The client repeats this 'walk' (steps 13–15) a few times.

17 'How is it now? What have you learnt?'

18 Future pace. 'What are you going to do different in the future?'

Example

The client is a man in his early fifties, seeking to make a big career change. Note: he has already had the process and its concepts explained to him.

Coach: Right ... So, what's the call to action? What are you being called to become or do?

Client: I would like to become a therapist.

Coach: What is the demon or challenge you must face?

Client: Self-doubt.

Coach: And how is that a problem to you now?

Client: I have a very nice career. On the surface anyway. Well paid, high status, all that sort of stuff. So there's this voice, nagging me, that I shouldn't give it up, because I'll make a mess of this new career direction.

Coach: Right ... What is the threshold? What is the unknown territory outside of your comfort zone that you'll have to enter in order to deal with this?

Client: It means for me changing my commitments in terms of managing my time and I'm going to have to maybe forgo certain things that I'd like, and that's something I've got to accept. It's a matter of believing in myself

the whole time, and this is very emotionally draining
… [*The client drifts off here: the coach does a brief piece of
rapport work, and gets him back into the process*]

Coach: Great! Now tell me, what resources do you need in
order to achieve this calling?

Client: I think my family will support me in this. My wife is
into this personal growth stuff, too, and our children
have left home – we had them pretty young … And I
know there are lots of good courses out there. It's just
me I've got to convince, really. That I can actually do
it … That's the demon. I need to stop self-doubting,
stop the critic in me, don't worry about the outcome
and just get on with the process.

Coach: I see that … Well, you don't have to deal with this
challenge alone. I'm going to ask who could be
mentors for you on the journey. They could be people
you know, famous people, now or in the past, people
in fiction – anyone you feel has that right energy that
could really help you succeed on this journey you're
making.

Client: Even made-up people?

Coach: Definitely.

Client: OK. I'd like a cartoon character called Atom Ant. Stupid,
really, but I used to watch the show as a kid, and I
always thought: 'He's tiny, but he's got amazing courage,
and doesn't let anything get in his way. Is that OK?

Coach: Of course.

Client: Good. Then I guess I'd better have a real person. My
dad was a wonderful example to me, and always said
I had to fight my own battles but that he'd be around
if anything went too badly wrong. I love that balance
of feeling encouraged to take risks, but there's a
kind of safety net somewhere. And a very loving one,
one that wouldn't say 'Told you so' but just love me
anyway.

Coach: That's lovely. Another mentor?

Client: I'm not sure.

Coach: Sometimes people like to choose a playful mentor, someone to lighten the load a bit.

Client: Yes, that's a good idea. I'd like a chipmunk. They're really playful and fun. [*Smiles*]

Coach: So if we had Atom Ant, your dad and a chipmunk, would that be OK? [*Moving on to the next section, mapping out the journey*] So – where is this past, present and future for you? Where's your line?

Client: Sort of here …

Coach: Great. We need a start point, the threshold, the demon, the mentors and the elixir. [*Client points to the present*] Great. Now where's the threshold, the thing you need to push past?

Client: It's actually quite close. [*Points*]

Coach: And the demon?

Client: I'd say it's just here.

Coach: And the mentors? You'll visit them before the demon because you want to get resources first. So lay them out on the timeline, to the left or to the right of the timeline. Atom Ant, your dad, the chipmunk. So where would you like them to be?

Client: I'm going to put Dad quite close to the demon. Atom Ant I'm going to put in the middle, and my chipmunk – perhaps I should put him here between the two …

Coach: Now what about the outcome you want?

Client: I'm going to just where the demon is, and I'll put it halfway between that and the wall.

Coach: Right, splendid. Now what I'd like you to do is answer this question: have you accepted your calling?

Client: Yes.

Coach: OK, lovely. Now what I'd like you to do is start walking to the threshold and just walk a little past it and notice what happens. Did you notice a little bit of resistance as you walked past the threshold?

Client: Yes, I did.

Coach: Where did you notice that in your body?

Client: Right here.

Coach: So let's do this strange role-play thing now. I'm going to push at you at that point ... [*Does this*] How are you going to get past me? You could push me, you could pull me, you could do anything that seems right to somehow overcome this resistance physically ...

Client: I'm just pushing back. That's going to be fine. You'll give in ... [*The client does this*]

Coach: So now you've passed the threshold. You're now in this strange, foreign land past the threshold. Yes?

Client: Yes.

Coach: The demon's over there, you've got your mentors. What I'd like you to do now is visit one of them. You can choose any of them that you like to visit first. So who would you like to go and hang out with?

Client: I'll visit Atom Ant.

Coach: So where's Atom Ant again?

Client: I think he was actually down here.

Coach: Just go into the character of Atom Ant. Be Atom Ant ...

Now as Atom Ant looking at Nick over there, just say what you need to say. You can say it out loud or say it silently, whichever you prefer.

Client: [*As Atom Ant, remember*] Up and at 'em! That was his catchphrase.

Coach: Now step in as yourself now, and receive that advice. [*Client does so*] Who do you want to visit next? [*Client goes to his dad and the chipmunk in turn, gets mentoring from them and then accepts it, as above*] Now as you walk forward towards the demon. What does the demon look like now? Describe him.

Client: I've got a set of tarot cards at home and every time you say demon the card of the devil comes up in my mind.

Coach: So that's still there, it's quite significant.

[The point here is that sometimes, once the mentors have been consulted and have given their resources, the demon shrivels up into nothing or even morphs into an ally. This has not happened here!]

Client: Yes.

Coach: Now I'd like you to be the demon. You might want to turn round and face Nick. Anything coming up?

Client: As the demon?

Coach: Yes.

Client: Full of self-doubt. Can I really go on with this?

Coach: Just stop there for a moment. Self-doubt has got a positive intention. What is your sense that the positive intention could be?

Client: To protect myself.

Coach: So knowing that, now step into the demon again. What do you need to tell Nick to make him feel safe?

Client: *[As demon]* Look after yourself.

Coach: Now, be Nick again. Receive whatever you need to receive … Now tell me what's happened to him.

Client: It makes sense. It'll be hard work – and emotionally draining. But I can be prepared for that stuff. I can take Dad's protection and the self-belief from Atom Ant. And I can laugh about things. I'll get through.

Coach: So is it possible to remove the demon from the line and put it somewhere so it can act as a further mentor for you?

Client: Yes.

Coach: Where would you like it to be?

Client: I'll put it there, the little devil!

[The coach now asks the client to 'do the walk' – up to the calling, where he sends a message back to the start. Then back

to the start, round the side of the room, where he receives the message. Then straight up along the timeline, past threshold, mentors, where the demon was, where the demon/mentor now is, calling, back round to the start again ... The client does this several times]

Coach: Do you want to do it again or was that enough?

Client: That was nice. I had a very positive affirmation at the end.

Coach: Anything you'd like to say to feel complete with this?

Client: No. I actually found the demon exercise the strongest: when I stood on it I actually felt more determination ... Once I got back that last time almost the sense was it's not that I'm 'going to do it' but 'it's done'.

The Hero's Journey

■ Based on the mythology research of Joseph Campbell

■ The client:

   ■ Identifies the calling

   ■ Accepts the calling

   ■ Crosses the threshold

   ■ Receives resources from mentors

   ■ Walks to the calling

   ■ Sends a message back to the start of the journey

   ■ Returns to that start and accepts the message

   ■ Walks past the threshold and the mentors and meets the demon

   ■ Walks the journey a few times, to get the learning firmly in place.

13

RESOLVING INNER CONFLICT

"'Pull yourself together' is seldom said to anyone who can."

Mignon McLaughlin, American writer and journalist

You will often find that clients seem incongruent over an issue, for example 'I hate my boss, but I must be nice to her or I will get the sack.' You will notice two 'characters' or *parts* emerging, one possibly angry and the other possibly scared. This uneasy mix of the two parts needs to be resolved. Being in this state of being pulled in two different directions by two different 'sub-personalities' is called being *simultaneously incongruent*.

In this chapter I shall present a process for dealing with these problems.

Parts Integration

The process begins with encouraging the client to sort the issue into *polarities* – two clear and discrete expressions of the warring feelings. The client then becomes *sequentially incongruent*.

Next, the coach encourages the client to give voice to one part using one hand, and then to give voice to the other part with the other hand. The client chooses which hand 'speaks' for which part. The two parts will soon assume characters, a bit like actors in a drama.

The client may not be at ease with the polarities that emerge, but at least now they can separate them. On the other hand, this simple act of *sorting* can often give a client a real boost – and if the client is up for it, you can intensify the sorting to emphasise the difference between the two parts.

■ **Sorting using calibration** – Notice the voice tone, gestures (etc.) of each part. Accentuate them.

■ **Sorting using rep systems and submodalities** – Encourage the client to create a picture and sounds for each part to gain greater clarity – Do the different hands feel different? If so, how? Can these be exaggerated?

■ **Sorting using psychological roles** – There are a number of psychological models you can use here. One is Virginia Satir's (see below). Another is the Parent, Adult or Child of Transactional Analysis (TA). Or another trinity from TA – Victim, Rescuer and Persecutor. If one of these models feels right, get each part further into their roles.

The Satir categories

Virginia Satir's work formed the basis of one of the original models for NLP. Among her many achievements was a model of five different roles people can slip into when faced by stress. These are:

■ **Blamer** – It's all someone else's fault! Aggressive with it.
■ **Placater** – This person often takes all the guilt on themselves, hoping that way to excite pity.
■ **Computer** – Distances themselves from the problem, goes all cold and uses long words to analyse the problem in some kind of theoretical way.
■ **Distracter** – Cracks a joke, suggests everyone goes down the pub … Also flips from one of the above roles to another one of them, so nobody can pin them down.
■ **Leveller** – Sees what is going on, accepts the emotional content of a situation and deals with it. Can create upset by 'telling it like it is'.

Having done this, the coach asks each part in turn for the *positive intention* behind its behaviour.

The desired outcome is that both parts understand:

- Their own positive intention
- The positive intention of the other part
- How both these intentions are necessary both to you as a whole individual human being and to both of the parts.

This can be a marvellously powerful exercise.

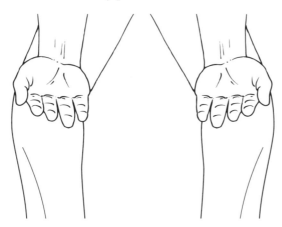

Step-by-step

1 Identify the conflicting parts and ask the client to choose which hand represents which part. If the client shows bias against one part, then take a respectful attitude to that part, which the client can then model. Later in the process it might be useful to ask the client to 'thank' or 'apologise' to that part.

2 Get a name for each part. Don't rush this – let the names emerge. Once you have them …

3 Touch a hand:

   (a) What does this one look like?

   (b) Any sound?

   (c) Any feel?

Break state.

4 Repeat steps 3 (a), (b) and (c) for the other hand.

Break state.

5 The client holds out both hands. Say: 'So, for once, you can look at both.'

6 Find out the positive intention of each part. It is usually preferable to start with the part that the client prefers. Point out one hand and ask, 'What is its positive intention for you?' or 'What does that part do for you?' It is advisable for the coach to point to the hand, or touch it gently, rather than use its name.

7 Then repeat for the other hand.

8 Have each part inform the other of its positive intention *for the other part*. Ask the client: 'What is this part's [*touch the relevant hand*] positive intention for this part [*touch the other hand*]?'

9 Then repeat for the other hand.

10 Have each part come to understand that it can only get what it wants with the aid of the other part.

11 Usually the person believes that the parts and the outcomes that each one desires are incompatible or totally irreconcilable. So 'chunk up', and ask the whole person: 'What is your positive intention?'

12 Integration. Use hypnotic language (see Chapter 15) to encourage the client to bring their hands together physically [*and, as they do this, to bring the parts together in the psyche*]. For example:

Drop inside and spend a few moments noticing how both are essential to you. And as you do, allow the two parts to come together in their time. Because it is not that you have choice of one or the other, you need both together and if teach them to cooperate, by BRINGING THEM TOGETHER NOW, you may well find as they come together that in this case one and one really make three. So just allow it to happen RIGHT NOW; bring together and notice how are both parts of you, finally working together, inside right now. And can you find a way to BRING THEM INSIDE YOURSELF FULLY and to allow the integration to take place RIGHT NOW. THAT'S RIGHT. Just allow yourself to enjoy that experience and notice any learnings you can take.

> This language may sound strange, but it is an effective way of talking 'directly' to the unconscious mind.

13 Having brought their hands together, the client may want to bring both hands to their chest and press against it, bringing the new understanding and positive intentions right into their heart. You can say as they do this: 'Take both these parts back inside you where they belong.'

14 Future pace.

There are of course many ways of sorting in this way. Fritz Perls, on whose work parts of this process were modelled, did it by having clients sit on two different chairs and 'being' the different parts, one on each chair. You can do it with simple geographical space. But the hands are sensitive parts of the body and can be brought together at the close of the exercise in a particularly satisfying and effective way.

Tips

I often add a section where I ask the client to hang one hand by their side and then ask them: 'What would life be like if you only had x [*the hand not hanging*]?' I do this for each hand, usually as part of step 10 in the process above. If the client is enthralled at the prospect and says 'Fantastic!', I ask what would ultimately happen if they had only that hand – and the answer usually becomes very negative. The client will then usually conclude that they need both, even if one is a counter to stop the other going too far.

In the final section of the process, clients often come up with imaginative ways of 'taking the parts back inside'. They can push hard into their chest, or even eat the parts! The motto here is 'whatever works' – encourage the client to do what is best for them, and not feel foolish. On the other hand, if they really don't want to do this, don't force it.

Finally, there is a philosophical learning from this process that I find useful sharing with clients. The human condition is structured by opposing voices. I have already mentioned Freud's Superego, Ego and Id and Berne's Parent, Adult and Child, but there are Jung's archetypes – King, Warrior, Lover and Magician – and the many subpersonalities in Roberto Assagloli's psycho-synthesis. When a client can accept that the strong and often negative feelings associated with one part is just how humanity operates, and then accept the positive intention of that part rather than struggle against it, life becomes much easier to live. Such an understanding can help people to 'make peace' with themselves.

"When a client can accept that the strong and often negative feelings associated with one part is just how humanity operates, life becomes much easier to live."

Parts Integration

The client:

- Identifies two conflicting parts of themselves
- Chooses a hand to represent each one
- Examines each in turn for its positive intention
- Enables each to realise the positive intention of the other
- Enables each to realise how it in some way needs the other
- Integrates both back into the 'whole person'.

14

BREAKING SPELLS AND FINDING A NEW WAY OF BEING

"Close the show and put a whole new show on the road."

Eric Berne, psychologist and founder of Transactional Analysis

Rescripting is a process I created myself. It is based on the work of Gregory Bateson, one of the founding fathers of NLP, who invented the concept of the *double bind* (later written about by RD Laing). A double bind is a pair of commands or injunctions or beliefs that pull someone in two opposing directions, so they are damned if they do and damned if they don't. They usually take the form of 'if *x*, then *y*; if not *x*, then *z*', where *y* and *z* are both undesirable outcomes. Examples are:

Work hard and be alone, or don't work hard and be unworthy.

If I am kind, I will be taken advantage of; if I am strong, no one will like me.

I found that in my own life, I had one of these that nagged at me:

If you do what you want, you will let people down and be worthless; if you don't do what you want, you will be miserable.

Such double binds are often transmitted down the generations in families and can have the quality of a 'family curse'.

The process also uses the concept of positive intention, and material from Transactional Analysis – Eric Berne believed that people wrote 'scripts' for themselves, which they then lived out; the purpose of this process is to reveal and then to rewrite these scripts, giving them a new, positive end.

I believe very strongly that maturity is about having your cake and eating it too – we can use, and can enjoy using, positive qualities such as ambition or drive without the need for compulsive, irrational behaviours.

The rescripting process

Part 1: the story

The client is asked to identify their favourite childhood story (*Sleeping Beauty, Little Red Riding Hood, James and the Giant Peach,* etc.). This is to get them in the mood for story-telling.

The client then suggests a positive character they can identify with (not necessarily from the story chosen above). This could be fictitious or real, King Arthur or Dorothy from the Wizard of Oz, Nelson Mandela or Anita Roddick.

The client then tells a story from that character's perspective – not the story of that character, but a story vaguely related to the story of the client's own family, starting at least with their grandparents and ending at the present day.

The point of telling the story this way is twofold. First, telling the story in the third person sets the imagination free and somehow allows the client an overview of the situation that is harder to get if they tell it as themselves. Second, they start with a character about whom they feel positive rather than ambivalent (which is probably how they feel about themselves, thanks to the double bind).

Magic can be used freely: if Berne is to be believed, we write our scripts when we are very young, and it is best to rewrite them in a child-like state.

Note that it is important that the client focuses on saying whatever comes into their mind without stopping. The aim is to get the story told, not to entertain the coach, who remains quiet and says nothing until the story ends, unless the client seems to get stuck, when the coach can intervene and say 'Keep going'. This is an exercise in rapport: can you remain present and curious and be with the client, without getting in the way? The client indicates when the story is over.

The coach asks the client to give a title to their story.

Part 2: the curse

The client is asked to identify their *family curse*.

The curse is summarised into a simple negative double bind. (Remember the shape: if x then y; if not x, then z, where y and z are both 'loser' outcomes.)

Work on this, so that it is in the right form and also as brief and 'punchy' as possible (as long as it is realistic). The more power the client puts into it (as long as it genuinely reflects their fears), the more forcefully the unconscious mind will be motivated to address the issue and the more effective and liberating its removal will be. Clients may fight this initially, and then end up with a resigned expression and say that it has a horrible familiarity to it. One simply told me it was 'home'.

Part 3: distilling the good of the curse into a metaphor

The client needs to congruently commit to giving up the curse today.

Having done this, it is time to look at the positive intention behind the curse. It is important for the client to highlight what they have achieved in their life. All their achievements – career, relationships, wealth, family – have been made with the curse in place, so it must have some benefits. (Often the x part of the curse is good advice – for example, the two curses I cited above, where x was 'work hard' and 'be kind'. It's what follows, the sting in the tail, that causes the problem.)

When they have established this intention, the client needs to think of a metaphor for them. The client will carry this into the new story, metaphorically honouring the positive intention behind the curse. Common examples of metaphors include a suit of armour, a golden key or magic shoes.

Part 4: the curse buster

The client is invited to continue the story from the present time to a future time when the curse is transformed. The metaphor can be used to destroy the curse, or is kept alongside the hero as a talisman (remember, we are dealing with stories worked out in childhood).

> Lancelot entered the water cave, where he was handed Excalibur by the watery maiden and destroyed the demon. He was led by the hand by the maiden to a bright beautiful garden, where he finally felt at peace.

> I went to a ball wearing the magic shoes, and met a prince. We fell in love and lived in small village, where we had a store and lived happily ever after.

The client then comes up with a name for their new story. Invite them to meditate briefly and to come up with one. A 'word' name is probably best, but they can choose anything – a sound, a picture, a gesture – as long as it works for them as an 'anchor' for the story.

Part 5: putting the new show on the road

The coach ensures that the following are all written down and agreed with the client:

- The name of the old story
- The name of the new story

- The carry-forward metaphor
- The curse itself.

Allow the client to make any changes and review these four concepts.

The client is invited to *mark out their timeline* so the coach knows where the past and future are represented spatially. The client is asked to point to their curse on the timeline.

The client is then asked to point to *all* occurrences of the curse, past and future. It is important to stress that they should point to how they perceive things to be now, not how they would like them to be.

If any occurrences of the old story are in the future, ask the client if it would be OK to move them all back into the past.

If the client shows any reluctance to moving them to the past, there is probably some aspect of the positive intention of the curse that is holding them back. Identify this and incorporate it into the carry-forward metaphor. Often, this will modify or add a new feature to their existing carry-forward metaphor. Then ask them again to move the occurrences into the past.

Ask your client if it would be OK for their new, alternative story (use its name) to be put on the timeline in their future. Ask them to place that tale on to their future in their own way. Finally, ask them to put the tale into their present.

Conclude by asking the client how things are now.

Rescripting: a scripted version

Part 1: the story

'What was your favourite story from childhood?'

'Think of a mythical, fictional, famous or movie character you might playfully like to identify with.'

'Tell me a story about this character that is vaguely related to the story of your family. Start at least as far back as your grandparents and end at the present day. You can use magic freely in this story. Say whatever comes into your mind without stopping. Focus on flow, not on entertainment value.'

'If you had to give this story a name, what would it be?'

Part 2: the curse

'Every family has a curse; what is your family curse?'

'Please summarise your curse into a simple negative double bind: "If x then y; if not x, then z."'

Part 3: distilling the good of the curse into a metaphor

'Are you willing to give up this curse today, if we can find an alternative story for you that enables you to maintain what is important to you?'

'There is something good this curse has done for you in the past, such as protection or motivation. What are the positive qualities of your curse?'

'Can you come up with a metaphor for these positive qualities, such as a suit of armour, a golden key or magic shoes?'

Part 4: the curse buster

'Now please continue the story from the perspective of your character from the present time, to a future time when the curse is transformed. You can use magic to transform the curse at the end. You may also want to use your carry-forward metaphor in this transformation ...'

'Allow yourself to go inside, now, and look for some words, pictures or feelings that will remind you of this transformation.'

Part 5: putting a new show on the road

'Let's write down the name of your old story, the curse at the heart of it, the name of your new story and your "carry-forward metaphor". Let me know if you want to change them in any way.'

'OK. Point to your future, then to your past: sketch out your timeline in the air for me.'

'Point to all occurrences of the curses past and future. Not where you want them to be, just where they are right now.'

[*If they are located in the future*] 'Would it be OK to move them back into the past?'

- ▪ *If 'Yes'* – 'OK, move them to the past.'

- ▪ If 'No' – 'What stops you?' [*Then find an alternative strategy to honour any positive intention*]

'Would it be OK for your new story, with a happy ending, to be put on the timeline in your future?'

'Great, place that tale into your future in any way you want. However you do it is just right.'

'Is there anything else you need to say or do to be complete with this process?'

'How is it now?'

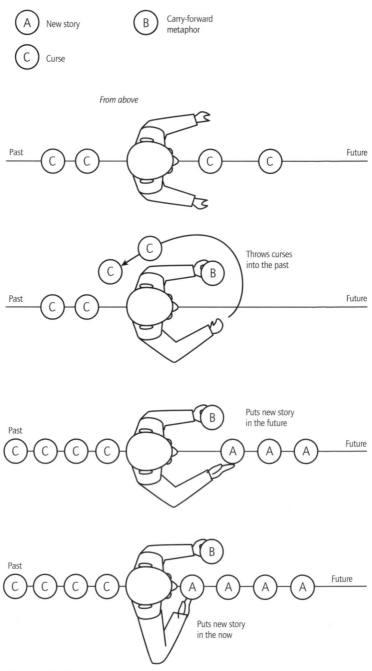

Diagram for Step 5

Rescripting

The client ...

- Identifies a favourite story from childhood
- Identifies a hero with hugely positive associations
- Tells a three-generation story from a third person perspective, and names the story
- Identifies a family 'curse'
- Creates a metaphor to carry forward what is useful from the past
- Creates a new story for the future, with a happy ending, and names the new story
- On a timeline, puts the old story in the past and the new story in the future
- Brings the new story into the present.

15

THE POWER OF HYPNOSIS

"Until you are willing to be confused about what you already know, what you know will never grow bigger, better or more useful."

Milton Erickson, hynotherapist

To teach hypnotic language is beyond the scope of this book. Or any book, actually: there really is no substitute for going on a course of NLP or hypnotherapy.

However, it's worth making a few points.

Hypnotic language is in many ways the opposite of the Meta Model introduced in Chapter 5. In that chapter, various ways in which clients misuse language were presented and shown as ways in to systems and structures in the client's mind. In hypnosis, the same misuses are found – but they are done deliberately, by the hypnotist. The listener finds themselves unable to understand, or at least make complete sense of, what is being said, and goes inside themselves to search for such sense. As they do this, they enter a state called *trance*.

In trance, clients can access unconscious resources. Remember the presupposition that 'clients already have all the resources they need' – their problem is that they have lost the ability to access these resources and are stuck in some kind of loop (or loops) of negative thoughts and behaviours. In trance, they can sidestep any loops and have a chance to rediscover these extra resources.

You can give your client both encouragement and guidance in their search. Encouragement comes from statements that remind them that they can make new connections and discoveries in the trance state. Hypnotherapists will often say things like 'And you can find yourself discovering all sorts of new things ...' Guidance comes via stories and metaphors that relate to the issues the client has brought to you.

The standard hypnotic story is about someone with the client's problems who then went and sorted them out. Clearly, the more subtly you can do this, the better. Milton Erickson was a master of this: see his book, *My Voice Will Go With You* for examples of how he crafted stories to free up troubled clients.

Hypnosis and society

Hypnosis has been much maligned by movies and popular culture, where it is associated with sinister characters like Svengali or stage hypnotism in which people are made to do silly things.

In fact, hypnosis is a common form of communication: story-tellers, advertisers, salespeople, politicians and religious leaders all use hypnosis as part of their repertoire (usually, they do this without knowing that they are so doing, and have learnt the techniques simply by trial and error). Trance is also a common state, and not only when mesmerised by one of the above. Holding a remote control in mid-air while watching TV, going into a quiet space in a lift and daydreaming are all forms of trance.

Hypnosis training enables you to use this material consciously, rather than in a haphazard way. And it will also teach you to spot attempts, conscious or otherwise, to get you into trance – not so that you never go into trance again, but so you can choose when to and avoid manipulation by others.

Embedded commands

The full art of hypnosis is a subject too big for this book. However, below I shall present a process that uses one particular hypnotic technique, that of the embedded command.

The embedded command is given by emphasising specific words in a sentence. This emphasis can be simply verbal, or it can be achieved by making eye contact with the person as you speak the chosen words. The classic example is the person who says:

> If you, LIKE ME, enjoy going to the seaside ...

The hypnotist is sending the message 'like me'.

Clearly, if this is done incompetently, it looks crass. And if it is done well but unethically, it is morally wrong. But if done subtly and in the service of the client, it is a powerful and ethical tool.

The process that follows uses embedded commands to overcome the client's sense that they do not have permission to do something (often to succeed). I often use it after the Well-Formed Outcome process presented in Chapter 7 – having decided on a goal and how to get there, some clients still need 'permission' to undertake the journey and take it to a satisfactory conclusion.

The Permission Pattern

This is a process that I have adapted for NLP from Transactional Analysis (TA). The original TA process, called Potency – Permission – Protection, was created by Claude Steiner in his work with alcoholics.

Note that at the end of the process, the coach 'sponsors' the client. The coach needs to genuinely want the client to succeed, believe they can succeed and, further, believe that by simply holding an intention for the client to succeed, they will actually assist in the process. I have found plenty of evidence that holding positive intentions for people does help them – as have the world's great religions, which advise us to pray for others. If you do not believe this, you can leave this section out – but if you can include this section in the process, it has great power.

Permission Pattern script

1 'What will this outcome do for you?'

2 'What will be the natural consequences if you do not follow this outcome?'

3 'What would happen ultimately if you do not follow this outcome?'

[*Continue to ask questions 2 and 3 until the client comes up with a significant negative long-term consequence. The client now has increased motivation to move away from this negative consequence and to move towards the outcome*]

4 'Please summarise your outcome in a very short phrase, often beginning with the word: "to". For example, it might be "To start my own business".'

5 'Is it OK if I ask you to give yourself permission to go for your outcome?'

6 (a) If the client says 'Yes', say 'OK, give yourself permission to GO FOR YOUR OUTCOME'. Create an embedded command at this point, by speaking the capitalised words a little louder, engaging the client with eye contact and leaning forward as you say them. The more subtly you can do this, the better. Note that if the client does not like the word 'permission', you can suggest 'allow yourself' or 'authorise yourself'.

(b) If the client says 'No', investigate why.

7 The client gives themselves the permission.

8 'How was that?' If the client is satisfied and appears congruent, go to step 10.

9 If the client is not satisfied, or says they are satisfied but do not appear congruent, say, 'I sense there was something missing; do you agree?' If the client agrees, identify the blocking issue and then find out the positive intention of that issue. Find an alternative source of whatever that positive intention brings. Then go back to step 6, and repeat until the client appears congruent and confirms this verbally.

10 'I want you to know that I will be holding a positive intention for you to succeed in your outcome, even though I will not physically be with you. I will also give you my email/phone number if you need to get in touch.'

11 'How is it now?'

12 'How will it be when you complete your outcome?'

Example

This is a continuation of the Well-Formed Outcome script in Chapter 7, with the same client, who wants to start his own business.

Coach: Please summarise your outcome in a very short phrase, often beginning with the word 'to'; for example, to be free and just do it, to start my own business, to be self-employed, something like that. How would you like to phrase it in your own words?

Client: To start my own business.

Coach: Is it OK to give yourself permission to start your own business? [*This is said in a straightforward, adult way*]

Client: Yes.

Coach: So give yourself permission to START YOUR OWN BUSINESS. [*Makes eye contact on the word 'start', leans forward and slightly emphasises the words in capitals*] And how was that?

Client: I give myself permission to start my own business. Yes. That feels good!

Coach: I want you to know that I'll be holding a positive intention for you to succeed and I'm going to be there for you. I'm going to give you a business card – here it is – and you can email me or call me whenever you want. I'm genuinely holding a positive intention for you to succeed and I mean that. So how is it now?

Client: Very positive. [*The client is nodding, has a large smile, wide slightly moist eyes and a slightly flushed complexion*]

Summary

The client:

- Identifies negative consequences of not acting

- Summarises the outcome into a very short phrase

- Confirms they want to give themselves permission

The coach:

- Gives an embedded command – 'Give yourself permission TO GO FOR YOUR OUTCOME'

- Offers sponsorship.

16

MASTERING NLP COACHING

"I have only one counsel for you – be a master."

Napoleon

Anyone can do it

Sometimes coaching is seen rather as the preserve of a certain type of person: while I don't think this is true, I do know that has put some people off coaching, and this is a loss to the world. NLP doesn't have the same problem. One of the things I like most about NLP is its inclusive feel. I get people from all walks of life on my courses at NLP School, and I really enjoy seeing a diverse group of people bonding and creating a great atmosphere.

You certainly don't need a medical background to be a great NLP coach. You do need curiosity, determination and a fundamental liking for people. Curiosity above all: I believe that the most competent people in the world are not necessarily those with qualifications but people who make the effort to learn something themselves, to take it apart and really understand how it works. These people are not bound by the rules and beliefs of the established order and develop a depth of understanding that can exceed that of those who have followed a 'school of . . .' approach. The NLP world is full of examples of individuals who have become amazing coaches through their own efforts, changing their own lives around, as well as the lives of their clients, using NLP as a channel for their interest in life and in people.

"You don't need a medical background to be a great NLP coach. You do need curiosity, determination and a fundamental liking for people."

Practice makes outstanding

(Not perfect. We are not seeking perfection!)

When I said above that people need to learn things themselves, I did not mean shut themselves away with books. Go on NLP and coaching courses. Meet fellow 'explorers' there and share learning. Attend NLP practice groups.

But none of the above will give you enough experience, essential as they are. If you are going to be truly fluent in the material in this book, you have to practise it, as a working coach, but first of all on yourself.

Working with yourself on this material will provide two benefits.

First, you will end up with your own 'internal coach', on call, 24/7. I remember one day, not long after I had started studying NLP, when I had to attend a very sick relative in hospital. I was so upset that I didn't think I could go inside, but I knew I had to. I sneaked off into some trees behind the main building and worked my way through the Circle of Excellence: it took about five minutes, after which I went into the hospital and handled everything. It wasn't pleasant, but it was OK.

Second, of course, it enables you to really get a process into the muscle before you attempt to use it with a client. This learning needs to be continuous. Even though I have been practising NLP for years, if I haven't used one of the processes for a few months, I can get a little rusty. Practising the process on myself, including walking around on bits of paper if necessary, enables me to refamiliarise myself with its subtleties and also to regain my enthusiasm for its effectiveness.

Flexibility and elegance

Remember NLP presupposition 5: 'In any interaction, the person with the greatest flexibility has most influence on the outcome.' Flexibility is a core value of NLP. (Cybernetics has been a big influence on NLP, especially W. Ross Ashby's law of requisite variety, which essentially states the above.)

At the same time, flexibility implies lots of options, and lots of options can become cumbersome, so NLP also cultivates an admiration for elegance, simplicity and flow.

These two sets of desirables could be seen as opposites, but actually if you keep them both in mind, you soon start developing both side by side. Remember Errol Flynn's bird again ...

Being able to hold a process lightly and to individually tailor that process to fit the client's needs and make that flow is coaching at its best. In order to obtain this level of flexibility and elegance, a good grounding in the processes I have covered is essential. Once you have learnt the processes inside out, they naturally become part of a repertoire.

"Being able to hold a process lightly and to individually tailor that process to fit the client's needs and make that flow is coaching at its best."

The best NLP coaches learn when to deploy a process formally, and have the client standing on bits of paper, and when to simply introduce an informal version of it discreetly into the ongoing coaching conversation, so the client is asked the questions that underlie the process. For example, using the Meta Mirror conversationally would involving asking questions such as:

■ **First position** – 'May I ask you a question from your perspective, for a moment forgetting what anyone else may or may not want – what do *you* want to have happen in this situation?'

- **Second position** – 'Now, although this might seem a bit odd, if you were to really put yourself in the shoes of "Joe", what would Joe want, from the way Joe sees the world?'

- **Third position** – 'I fully understand how significant this issue is for you. Can we try something a bit different? Pretend you saw two strangers and you overheard a conversation between them, very much like the one you and Joe had. What advice would you offer the "you" in that conversation to make the encounter less charged?'

Beyond this, of course, the master NLP coach creates their own processes, tailoring each one to the client and the client's need at that moment.

Taking it all further

NLP and developmental psychology

One of the key influences on cutting-edge NLP is the integral work of Ken Wilber and the Spiral Dynamics work of Don Beck and Chris Cowen. This essentially brings developmental psychology, and sociology, into NLP.

The concept that people evolve through different stages as they age is a well-known principle, and attempts at defining these stages have been made by many thinkers: Freud, Erik Erikson and Daniel Levinson are probably the best known.

Wilber, Beck and Cowan have come up with a model that has been particularly taken on by NLP.

The Spiral Dynamics model looks at the evolution of both societies and individuals and posits that both follow a similar pattern. This pattern is a constant change from a focus on the individual to a focus on the collective – though the model doesn't just suggest a kind of pendulum, endlessly swinging from one to the other, but adds an upward motion, so on returning to an individualistic position, a person or a society has evolved a subtler version of its earlier individualism.

The key principle of this model is that as we grow up, we pass through stages. These stages can overlap. They have been given colour names for ease of use:

Beige – Individual survival, learning basic motor skills – 0–5 years

Purple – Magical, trying to understand cause and effect – 6 months to 5 years

Red – Asserting ourselves, the terrible twos to the rebellious adolescent – 2–18 years

Blue – The adolescent powerful desire to 'belong', as part of either a conformist or non-conformist group, believing there is only one true way to be – 11 years onwards

Orange – Asserting ourselves as we enter the world of work, wanting to live the good life and becoming more flexible and opportunistic – 16 years onwards

Green – A move towards a more inclusive world view, with environmentalism, positive activism and often alternative spirituality – 16 years onwards

Yellow – In this stage, we begin to transcend the individual/ collective pendulum and can combine the caring, sharing mindset of green with a hard-headed capacity for organising both ourselves and other people efficiently and effectively. We have the capacity for tough love and can provide truly inspirational leadership.

Beyond this, the material becomes more speculative and is based on societies and individuals that are yet to emerge. I find it best to focus on the established stages above.

From a psychological perspective, if there was trouble passing through a stage, such as overly logical parents who didn't permit fantasy during the Purple phase or controlling parents who did not permit self-expression during the Red phase, this can taint someone in later life. The person blocked at the Purple phase may be susceptible to join cults, and the individual who had Red suppressed may have issues around anger or asserting boundaries.

Techniques such as New Light Through Old Windows and Rescripting can resolve such issues.

More generally, much coaching is about helping people make transitions, and I find this model helpful in looking at the kinds of transition people may be wrestling with. Clients are often at some kind of crisis point, where one way of living in the world is beginning to prove unsatisfactory but they have not yet found a new one that suits them. The Spiral Dynamics model provides both direction and reassurance that the transition will work out.

Mind, body and spirit

A client may be frustrated with their body, unable to express themselves physically; they may have a deep urge to connect to some higher purpose or have some kind of spiritual experience. If one or both of these longings is or are not satisfied within a client, then an unhealthy expression of these needs is likely to manifest itself. But coaching and traditional NLP are very much focused on the mind. Often coaches will attract clients who have spent years exploring their mind and will get minimal results, as they end up going over the same old stuff. The master NLP coach needs to expand beyond a purely mental focus.

It is a well-known aphorism in coaching that 'a client is limited by the beliefs of their coach'. If you as a coach do not believe in any kind of spirituality or do not value the physical aspects of life, then this will impact your clients.

On the physical side, a client's health, vitality and sexuality are essential components of wellbeing. The good coach will ensure the client looks after themselves in these areas.

On the spiritual side, many people need some kind of connection to something bigger than, and outside, themselves. (This is not, by the way, an attempt to evangelise: I was not raised to follow any specific faith and I do not follow one now, though I do meditate regularly and enjoy a sense of connection to spirit, which is very personal.)

Every society in history has had spiritual components, but since the Industrial Revolution these elements have been increasingly discounted by science. Industrialised societies prospered and dominated so-called 'less developed' ones; spirituality came to be seen as superstitious and backward. Modernism, the dominant intellectual paradigm of the twentieth century, was firmly atheistic and viewed spirituality as at best comic. Philosophers such as William James who took spirituality seriously were sidelined. This attitude was shared by the founders of NLP: it took later NLP thinkers such as Robert Dilts and Stephen Gilligan to introduce a spiritual note into the discipline.

As a result of these attitudes, many people have had spirituality drummed out of them in childhood: 'Grow up; get a proper job; be rational…' (For other people raised in a religious tradition, spirituality has withered under the onslaught of tedious sermons and lists of life-denying 'don'ts'.) The yearning that is left can be manipulated by cults.

For the above reasons, there is a lack of wisdom in our society that used to be offered by traditional religious teachers, and some people are now looking to coaching and contemporary NLP to make up for this lack.

There's a danger here that people with NLP skills and personal charisma can turn into gurus. But there is also an opportunity for the sensible, caring NLP coach to help clients, by gently pointing them in directions that they may find helpful.

In the Coach to Awakener model, this is awakening. Perhaps that's a rather grand term – it makes me think of blowing a trumpet in the ear of a sleeping person. But a more gentle awakening can come first by simply acknowledging the importance of the spiritual dimension, and then by offering to teach meditation techniques or by helping clients to give themselves permission to take time out of their busy lives to spend time in nature or listening to music. The coach is not there to 'push' any route – whatever one the client chooses is right for them.

Also, by taking these issues seriously yourself (without evangelising), you demonstrate an attitude they can 'model' if they choose to. In a busy, cynical world, that in itself can be of huge value.

The Field Mind

This term was created by Stephen Gilligan. While it is quite a speculative concept, it is also open to an attractively wide range of interpretations.

The Field Mind is essentially some kind of intelligence beyond the human individual.

This can be thought of as an 'emergent' property of a group of people – or even two people, such as coach and client. The healing properties of the coaching 'space' are the result of some kind of synergy where something bigger than the two individuals comes into being.

The phenomenon of *limbic resonance* is perhaps another example of this. When two mammals interact, say a man stroking a cat, studies show that at a certain point their physiologies begin to mirror each other. It's as if the mind/body systems of the two beings have in some sense merged. See *A General Theory of Love* by Thomas Lewis, Fari Amini and Richard Lannon for more on this.

Taking the idea further, the psychologist Jung talked of a 'collective unconscious', a shared existence where humans connect with or share archetypal qualities. And, of course, traditional religions – except perhaps some strains of Buddhism – all posit a cosmic intelligence far superior to our own.

As with all NLP, our ultimate interest in this concept is how useful it is: even if we do not agree on what the Field Mind is or how it works, there seem to be powerful causes at work that are not products of purely individual mind-work, and some of these are relevant to coaching.

Personally, I find believing in the existence of a Field Mind a great comfort. It is effectively a content-free form of *faith*. The belief helps me accept what happens in a less controlling and more curious way. It provides a shared sense of sprit without the exclusivity problems that different religions seem to create.

NLP coaching contexts

In this final section, I shall look at NLP coaching in three contexts where it is most commonly used commercially: the field of business, life coaching, and sports/performance coaching. I shall also discuss informal coaching among friends and family.

17

NLP COACHING IN THE WORKPLACE

"Most of what we call management consists in making it difficult for people to get their work done."

Peter Drucker

Using the coaching mindset as a manager

The skills of coaching are very useful for the modern manager. Being able to hold space and listen, being able to ask pertinent questions and offer suggestions in a constructive way – these things can truly energise staff and help them gain confidence. When this approach is applied to already motivated workers, people can begin to take more responsibility, which then frees the manger from the time-consuming business of micro-management.

Managing highly performing individuals can be similar to the caricature of the manager of celebrities, whereby you provide a listening space where they can unburden their concerns and leave feeling relieved and ready for the next task at hand. The coaching approach is ideal for this kind of challenge.

Understanding the metaprogrammes of staff at all levels can lead to huge improvements in morale, as you will now know how to recognise and acknowledge good performance in different individuals.

Project planning can be greatly assisted by using the NLP Creativity Process described in Chapter 11, either formally or, for staff not used to NLP, informally, wearing the three 'hats' of Dreamer, Realist and Critic when discussing ideas.

Yet management is not the same as coaching. The manager has an overt agenda, to make sure people get their work done.

If the boundaries of coaching and management get blurred, problems can occur. Managers can fall in love with coaching and end up 'playing doctor'; ten-minute meetings with staff members turn into fascinating but unproductive two-hour 'sessions'. Although this sort of thing is relatively harmless from time to time, too much of it can waste resources. If you are a manger who loves coaching, find some clients in your spare time.

Problems can also arise if staff seek coaching from you on sensitive issues. An element of mentoring has always been part of really good leadership, but the wise manager knows where to draw the line.

At a broader level, companies can embrace a coaching culture by creating in-house coaching, where members of the human resources department are trained to coach, so staff are coached or mentored by individuals who they do not directly report to. This can go wrong if the training is inadequate, or if the new 'coaching' team does not have access to good external supervision. I feel that this kind of solution is an uneasy compromise.

The best solution is to bring in external executive coaches. Of course, as such a coach myself, I have an agenda for saying this. But I do genuinely believe this to be the best solution. Professional executive coaches are experienced, both in coaching in general and in the subdiscipline of executive coaching. They are used to dealing with issues of confidentiality and know where to draw these difficult lines.

Executive coaching

> Over-seriousness is a warning sign for mediocrity and bureaucratic thinking. People who are seriously committed to mastery and high performance are secure enough to lighten up.
>
> Michael J. Gelb, American writer and trainer

Executive coaching is three-sided, involving the *coach*, the *client* (the person being coached) and the organisation (or, more specifically, the *manager* from whose budget the coaching is coming; such a person is often called the sponsor, but I won't use this term, to avoid confusion with sponsoring in the sense used in the Coach to Awakener model).

Ideally the following sequence of events will occur:

1 The client and the manager meet before the coaching session and agree a set of outcomes. The more that can be clarified in this session, the better.

2 Client, coach and manager meet and discuss and further clarify this list. Requirements can still be rather vague ('He needs to improve his communication style') and need to be made more specific ('He needs to make his presentations more engaging'). There are also likely to be specific goals that the client is working towards that can be added to the list.

  These meetings can sometimes descend into something like relationship counselling where both parties have a row in front of the coach. This can be due to unhelpful suggestions from the manager ('Can you make him stop being such a difficult so and so …') – often this is a result of not having had the previous manager/client meeting. If this happens, it's best to take control and say something like 'There are obviously issues here – let's make a note of that and move on.' You certainly now have important material to work on!

  This meeting is also a time for the coach to make sure that both parties understand how modern coaching works. Some managers still see coaching as traditional sports coaching, where the coach tells the client how to become better at things. The coach needs to explain tactfully that, while there is an element of teaching (coaching at the level of capabilities) in NLP coaching, the exercise is a much broader and deeper thing than that. (Such a view on behalf of a manager is not to be treated with disrespect: the average person still associates coaching with men in tracksuits with whistles. Such a manager needs to be shown, with enthusiasm, how far things have moved on.)

3 The coach and client have their first session, where the contract is created. The contracting is similar to the material covered in this book, with the addition of a discussion of the requirements of the manager. Two lists of areas of primary focus are created – one that the client sends to the manager, and that can be benchmarked against progress at the end of the coaching sessions, and a second one, that will contain additional confidential issues that will not be shown to anyone else, just coach and client.

4 After the first session, it is worth trying to schedule the remaining sessions straight away. But be aware that many busy executives cancel coaching at the last minute. Applying strict cancellation terms can help discipline the worst offenders.

5 The final session will involve helping the client to prepare a report for the manager or arranging a further three-way meeting.

A number of issues can arise from executive coaching.

Although strictly speaking the coach is contracted to work entirely for the client, the organisation writes the cheque and conflicts of loyalty can emerge. Examples are managers who tell you confidentially that your client will be 'heading for the door' regardless of the coaching outcome, and clients who tell you that they have already accepted another job and want to use the coaching to address other issues.

Another problem can be when a conflict-averse manager uses the coach to do their job, getting you to deliver bad news or to deliver comments about the client's work. This is not the job of the coach: if you do find yourself in this position, the best thing to do is point this out, politely of course, to the manager.

Sometimes the coach can find themselves in an organisation whose culture they dislike.

In all these cases, the coach needs to exercise judgement. There is an inevitable element of unease in the three-sided relationship that is executive coaching, and part of the skill of the job is to deal with this. But if there comes a point where you feel your integrity is being significantly compromised, you can always walk away. In the end, organisations tend to value coaches with integrity. If you compromise your coaching principles, you may get short-term gain (or relief from short-term annoyance), but in the long term you cheapen yourself. 'Firm but polite' is the motto.

On a more personal level, coaching can overinflate people's ambitions or their colleagues' expectations of them. This is the flip-side of the coaching sceptic: the person who thinks it is a magic wand. If coaching makes someone rush into a job that they are actually not ready for, then it does them no favours. Watch out for this excessive faith, and inject realism into the proceedings where appropriate.

Despite the difficulties outlined above, my experience is that most organisations, although not perfect, are reasonable in their approach. When executive coaching is done well, and the staff member is willing and able, it is an extremely effective form of development, with wins all round for coach, client and manager.

Team coaching

> When a team outgrows individual performance and learns team confidence, excellence becomes a reality.
>
> Joe Paterno, American football coach

This is a growth area within business coaching. Team coaching can transition a team quickly out of the 'storming and norming' phase towards the 'performing' phase. (It is also a lucrative source of clients, as individuals often request individual coaching after such events.)

Team coaching can take a number of forms, but I recommend the following stages:

1 Discussions with the team leader

2 Individual sessions with each participant

3 Areas of primary focus agreed

4 Team-building event

5 Follow-up coaching.

In the first stage, the team leader will give their views on each member of the team (these may or may not be helpful). It is important for the coach to be able to recall these observations, without necessarily buying into them. The coach needs to explain coaching to the team leader, and to make it clear that the best team coaching is a team event, not something driven by the leader.

In the next stage, the coach meets each member of the team individually, typically for around 45 minutes. A further piece of contracting around confidentiality is required: some of their comments will be fed back to the leader but made anonymous so it could not be attributable to them.

The coach then shares this confidential, non-attributable feedback to the leader and together they identify the areas of primary focus for the event and agree a coaching programme for the away session.

The event itself is best done in a new environment and involving an overnight stay – costlier but much more effective. An ideal structure is:

1 Early evening, explain – and redefine, if that proves necessary – the outcomes for the event

2 Some social time over a meal and then an early night

3 A full day going through various exercises.

The team works through the outcomes, breaks them down, and attempts to solve them, or at least agrees steps for their future resolution. The coach ensures that clear lines of responsibility and deadlines are drawn.

The Seven Parallels exercise, described below, makes an ideal template for the day. Participants will be expected to share their thoughts – the values section is often particularly powerful, both the individuals' personal values and their perception of what the values of the organisation are.

At the end of the process, a team will usually have clear goals and a vision they have co-created, which can be highly motivating.

The Seven Parallels

This helps people both align their own Logical Levels and check where there is a good or bad fit between these and the Logical Levels of their organisation.

The process is reasonably self-explanatory: the client fills in the form below for themselves and then for the organisation as they see it. It can be done as 'homework'.

The client needs to have some understanding of the Logical Levels to do this. If the Coach to Awakener model has been explained to them, this should suffice:

- **Mission** – Many organisations have mission statements, so just enter that here (even if it is very bland). Discussion along the lines of 'Great, but what really is the mission of the company?' can be useful.

- **Identity** – For the organisation's identity, I suggest a positioning statement, which is a narrow, objective assessment of what market the business is in and where it stands in that market, for example: 'We are number two in the UK biofuels industry'. But the client has to come up with their own metaphors, both for themselves and for the organisation. This is often hugely telling.

- **Values** – Organisations sometimes list official values, but it is more helpful if the client works out their own interpretation of the organisation's values from how things are actually done there.

- **Desires** – These are not a traditional part of the Logical Levels, but they are important in this exercise. The individual's answer to this should be related to what they want *from* work, though this doesn't have to be about what they want *at* work: in other words, an answer such as 'Enough money to have a good lifestyle for my family' is entirely appropriate.

- **Skills** – I have divided the personal side into four aspects: initiative, technical, self-management and interpersonal. Technical and interpersonal skills are obvious. People in some jobs may feel there is little scope for initiative – but rate yourself for this anyway (if you feel there is a big gap between your capacity for initiative and your current work, maybe it's time to use some of that initiative to change jobs).

- **Self-management** – This is about what Peter Senge calls 'personal mastery', the extent to which you understand

	Self	**Organisation**
Mission		
Identity	Three top identity statements in order: Metaphor:	Positioning statement: Metaphor:
Values	Three top values in order: 1 2 3	Three top values of the business: 1 2 3
Desires	I want:	The business needs:
Skills (*Grade yourself*)	Self-starting 1_____10 Technical 1_____10 Self-managing 1_____10 Interpersonal 1_____10	Leadership 1_____10 Operations 1_____10 Finance/legal 1_____10 Sales/marketing 1_____10
Goals	Goal 1: *Date* Goal 2: *Date* Goal 3: *Date*	Goal 1: *Date* Goal 2: *Date* Goal 3: *Date*
Assets (*Grade yourself*)	Physical 1_____10 Human 1_____10 Financial 1_____10 Intellectual 1_____10	Physical 1_____10 Human 1_____10 Financial 1_____10 Intellectual 1_____10

yourself, value what is best in you and are working on those aspects you realise are weaknesses.

- **Assets** – These are reasonably self-explanatory. By 'human assets', I mean the quality (and to a lesser extent quantity) of your links to other people: your family, close friends, other contacts. Note that this section is best filled in based on your entire life, not just at work – though it can be interesting to do two gradings, one for yourself as a whole and one for the person you 'bring to work'. While I think the idea of 'bringing your whole self to work' is a little idealistic, leaving too much at home is a recipe for lack of fulfilment: if this exercise reveals your work self to be a shadow of your full self, this is useful learning and something to work on.

Business owner coaching

Are you working in the business or on the business?

Peter Drucker

Because I am an entrepreneur as well as a coach and have written on the subject, I am often approached by other entrepreneurs for coaching. This can be an unusual and interesting dilemma. They present themselves as a business client, but their business and their life are completely enmeshed – no 'leaving your true self at home' for entrepreneurs – and my work becomes a mixture of executive coaching, consultancy and life coaching.

They start by saying they are looking for a sounding board for issues within their business. However, many entrepreneurs already have many sounding boards: staff, professionals (solicitors, accountants), partners, friends, etc. I often sense these clients actually want something more but are too proud to ask. The problem with this is if, as a coach, you act as simply yet another sounding board, these clients will get bored and impatient – something that happens very quickly with many entrepreneurs – and they will probably stop the coaching. On the other hand, if you try to press them down a personal development route, they may dislike the lack of control – another common entrepreneur trait – and also stop the coaching.

The approach that I have found works is that in the contracting session I lay out my stall, discussing options such as NLP. Entrepreneurs are often curious and up for trying new things: they tend to be excited by this and end up taking to NLP like a duck to water.

A few words of warning. Most entrepreneurs I have met are mismatchers on their metaprogrammes: they have made a good living by questioning the consensus. Therefore, whatever you suggest, they will put up a counter-argument – that is their nature. You will probably find you have to prove your mettle each time you meet.

One thing you can guarantee: the sessions won't be dull!

18

NLP LIFE COACHING

"The good life is inspired by love and guided by knowledge."

Bertrand Russell, philosopher

Life coaching, where clients want you to use your NLP coaching skills to help them resolve various personal issues, can be particularly satisfying. Typical issues include weight loss, relationships, quitting smoking and anxiety, and I will look at each of these in turn.

First, a couple of general points.

In this type of coaching, the first session is often taken over by a long life history of the client. This is understandable, as the client often gets huge benefit from this, and up to a point is a good thing – take notes during this unburdening. But don't let the contracting disappear – it is the key to all good coaching.

Over time, it is good to assemble an array of facts about certain issues that you can use to challenge clients' false beliefs. A good example is quitting smoking. Clients may believe that the physical effects of giving up are 'extremely painful'. But this can be questioned. The exact nature of addiction can not be defined, as the boundaries between psychological habit and physical dependence are impossible to delineate. The fact that people do not wake up in the middle of the night to obtain a fix of nicotine demonstrates that the physical dependence is often overstated. As your client has some control over the psychological aspects, minimising their belief in the power of the physical empowers them to quit. Chipping away at unhelpful beliefs like this one is a key part of life coaching, and having facts at your fingertips to help you do this is very useful.

Weight loss

It is worth beginning with some reframing. The term 'weight loss' is unhelpful; refer to the issue as 'body shape' instead. This is because fat weighs less than muscle, and so highly beneficial visits to the gym will actually increase weight initially.

The Well-Formed Outcome is very useful here. In the section that enables the client to imagine the goal, use some mild hypnotic language to ask them to imagine looking a certain way, perhaps recalling a memory and having once felt vital, flexible and fit.

The 'positive by-product' section often reveals an underlying emotional reason such as a need for comfort, or an unconscious wish to stay safe by repelling potential suitors. If issues such as these arise, it can be worth using some of the more powerful NLP interventions such as the Hero's Journey, Parts Integration or Rescripting to resolve limiting beliefs or enhance the client's sense of self. Clients wary of NLP will need to be paced and led into these intense processes: they can be encouraged to learn to trust you, and NLP, over a few sessions with some gentler processes.

Examination of values will often show that some clients simply value food and drink more than their body shape. They have to decide whether they want to change this.

Clients can learn new capabilities for monitoring their physical state. People with consistent body shapes don't just look at the bathroom scales, but also assess themselves by how they look and feel, and adjust their diet and exercise regime quickly if any of these criteria tell them they are going off track.

In the process of Mapping Across, comparing fit with 'stuffed and sick' can also plant some useful unconscious new behaviours into a person's lifestyle.

Other clients may be further down the line – they have sorted out the deeper issues and simply need help planning exercise and learning to count calories. Other useful behaviours clients can learn is to eat only when they are hungry, to stop eating when they are full (leave food on your plate regardless of what your parents told you), and to eat slowly so they can savour the food and give their body time to send 'I'm full' signals to their brain.

I have found discussing some of the facts around the fairly common practice of fasting to be helpful. One- and three-day fasts, building up to seven-day fasts, can be beneficial to health. Before undertaking these longer fasts it is best for the client to consult a physician and check they don't have any conditions that would make fasting unwise. Try reading *The Miracle of Fasting* by Paul and Patricia Bragg; the style is something of an acquired taste, but there is interesting material in there. They count Clint Eastwood among the many thousands of clients who have successfully used their methods for over 40 years.

Relationships

Clients may be grieving at the end of a particular relationship. Sometimes the job of coach is simply to listen, and maybe to point out that grief is a natural and healthy reaction to loss, which will pass over time. An issue that is more structural and thus more suited to coaching is that of people who keep 'picking bastards/bitches' or who keep messing up relationships themselves.

As usual, the Well-Formed Outcome can be of great assistance. This process can be a quite easy journey to some simple, sensible goals, but it can also dig deep in the by-products section.

The Rescripting process is very powerful for resolving painful issues around desirability and worth and can put an end to seeking out abusive partners.

After the big issues have been sorted out, coaching can be more practical. (Note here that the powerful process ideally comes in the middle of the coaching, as there is practical work to be done after it.)

I often talk to clients about the roles they play, or want to play, in their life. One role most of us want is that of 'partner'. Unattached clients respond to that by saying that's not a role you can choose; if you have no partner, you can't play it. I point out that the role is rather bigger than just being with someone. It is actually a cycle: I can express my role as partner by looking for a relationship, by building and maintaining a relationship, and by honouring and grieving the end of a relationship. Simply by going online and looking at singles adverts, you are playing the opening part of that role. The middle part of partnership is 'making an effort' in your relationship with another person, and you can practise this in your existing non-sexual relationships or during dating. And you can look back and mourn lost relationships, too. So, instead of being irredeemably stuck outside the world of partnership, singles are actually just at a different phase in the partnership cycle. Clients find this piece of reframing very helpful.

A client who had been divorced for a number of years and had not had a relationship since was fearful of dating. Partly this was because she was 'out of practice', but there was also a positive, protective intention: 'If I start dating, I may fall in love and get hurt again'. The client stated that intimacy was one of her highest values in life.

We used the process of Parts Integration, with one hand being loneliness and the other fear of rejection. These quickly turned into 'protection' and 'love'. Concentrating on protection enabled her to create various strategies to look after herself once dating started.

We also did the Circle of Excellence, an ideal process to boost confidence and make the process fun rather than a grisly ordeal (a mindset that, of course, makes a person more attractive).

Smoking

This material can also be used for drinking and drugs.

Begin with a vital question: Do you want to give up smoking? Often this is met with an incongruent 'Yes'. I then point this out to the client and ask whether they feel they *should* give up smoking or whether they really *want* to give it up. If the client says 'I really should stop, but I don't want to', it is generally best if they come back when they genuinely want to quit. However, the realisation that they are not sincere, combined with knowing they have taken the time and trouble to get coaching over the issue, can often shift them very quickly to making a clear, motivated decision to quit.

Once this has happened, it is useful to start with the Well-Formed Outcome, where the goal of giving up smoking (away from) can be reframed into something like 'to live a long healthy life'.

It is good to help the client imagine a healthy body, using all the rep systems: seeing clean fingers and teeth, hearing clear breathing, smelling flowers or enjoying the taste of food. A whining internal voice saying 'This is damaging my health' can be replaced with a more positive message. These visualisations are very powerful as most people can remember times without smoking that have many positive associations.

It is important to run through the positive by-products and produce a list. Often smokers are initially reluctant to admit to the practice having any positive benefits, but after a bit of badgering quite a long list can emerge.

I invite the client to consider the issue at the level of identity. I have already described a common scenario on page 93, where smoking has become associated with adult identity but can easily be challenged. This is remarkably common.

Some smokers enjoy the drama of 'giving up' and then starting again, but compared with the big issues of life it really isn't a big deal objectively. A word from a great coach – my dad, an ardent smoker who finally gave up, 'The good thing about giving up smoking is you don't have to worry about giving up smoking anymore.'

Collapsing Anchors

A useful NLP process to use in combating nicotine addiction is Collapsing Anchors.

Smokers will have a set of triggers that set them off doing it – anchors, in NLP parlance. The aim of this process is to interrupt the triggering process by inserting a set of new, positive associations into the old process whereby we felt craving and reached for the cancer sticks.

To make this work, the positive associations have to be powerful enough to outweigh the existing negative ones.

In this example, I apply the anchor by touching the client's knee. Obviously this touching has to be agreed with the client.

1   Ask the client to recall a memory when they were really healthy and had a great sense of vitality, clear breathing and smelling something pleasant (hiking among flowers is perfect). Ask them which knee they want to associate that memory on to. This will be 'knee 1' in the process.

2   Ask the client if they wish to close their eyes and then ask them to re-enter the positive memory. When they are fully associated with the memory, press knee 1 with your finger and say, 'See what you see, hear what you hear and feel what you feel.' Keep this pressure on, until it seems the memory has 'peaked'.

3   Test the anchor: quickly and covertly replace your finger on the exact spot and ask, 'Did that bring back a mild sense of that

memory or state?' If not, repeat step 2 until the touch alone triggers the memory or state.

4   Now ask the client to imagine a time when they really hated the fact they smoked. Perhaps they had trouble breathing or there were unpleasant smells. They may have been saying something like 'Smoking is really worrying me.' Repeat step 2, on the client's other knee (knee 2).

5   Touch knee 2 and say, 'Do you want this? Or ...' (now touch knee 1 as well) '... do you want this? You can have either. Which do you want?'

6   Hold both, equally strongly, for as long as required. The client will usually finally say they want 'that one' (the flowers). At that point, remove the pressure from knee 2 (the smoking association). Notice the positive response in the client, and then remove pressure from knee 1.

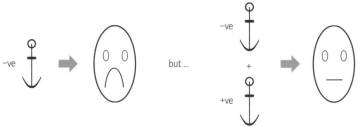

Collapsing Anchors

Anxiety and negative emotions

The NLP approach to these is essentially to examine the strategy, in as minute detail as possible, that the client uses to end up in these states.

Remember from Chapter 4 that a strategy in NLP is simply a mental computer program made up of units of attention. There is no implication that the client has deliberately set out to depress themselves. The idea can be 'sold' to the client by saying something like:

Would it be useful to find out the precise mental process you go through that ends in feeling depressed, so you might be able to find an alternative?

For example, a client worries whenever they leave the house that they have forgotten to lock the back door.

Coach: Can you go into more detail, please? What exactly happens?

Client: Well, I see a picture of myself forgetting to lock my front door. Then I say to myself, 'Someone could break in and break up all my things and they may lie in wait for me.' Then I feel a pounding sensation in my head and say, 'I must go back and check.'

Coach and client can then choose ways of interrupting this process. For example, the client could promise themselves that whenever they see their front door in their mind's eye, they will ignore it.

In this process you are acting as a teacher, showing the client how to become aware of their negative inner dialogue and for them to act as their own coach.

The Meta Model, presented in Chapter 5, can be of great use in this process. For example, this client is afraid of going into work:

Client: I am worried they won't like me.

Coach: Worried who won't like you?

Client: People.

Coach: Which person?

Client: Sarah.

Coach: How do you know Sarah doesn't like you?

Client: She doesn't look at me.

Coach: Do you always look at people you like?

Client: No.

Coach: So how do you know specifically that she doesn't like you?

Client: I guess I don't.

Clients who have gloomy thoughts can learn to develop new strategies using positive anchors. Encourage them to anchor each enjoyable part of their day – even (or, actually, especially) small things, like enjoying a cup of tea or smiling at someone on a bus. Getting someone to focus their attention on the positive can be very life-affirming.

"Clients who have gloomy thoughts can learn to develop new strategies using positive anchors."

Clients can also learn how to do meditation patterns, especially the abdominal breathing part of the Three Tyres exercise. This will help them relax rapidly from strong feelings of anxiety or anger.

It is also useful to steer the client away from labelling themselves as 'depressed'. While this can be consoling – the client can say they have an illness rather than think that they are doing something 'wrong' – it is not empowering in the long term. Nearer the truth, in my view, is the claim that a part of them is trapped in a depressed state. An exercise like Parts Integration can help the client look at this part, come to terms with it and make the changes they need.

It is at times like this when the coach's humanity, integrity and trustworthiness come to the fore: the part may not say 'nice' or politically correct things, but it needs to be witnessed by the coach. Often, when it has had its rant, it will change.

I have already made this point in discussing these 'big' techniques, but a reminder is perhaps appropriate here: if you do not feel up to this, that's fine. Refer the client to a therapist and work on other things with the client.

Arguably, NLP tools fall into two types: those that help people manage their own states and those that in some way transform original, troubling experiences. The former are easier to use and learn, so start with these. Curious and creative clients will enjoy learning new methods to manage their state – and knowing that this can be done is, of itself, highly liberating.

NLP COACHING IN OTHER AREAS

"Fatigue makes cowards of us all."

Vince Lombardi, American football coach

Sports coaching

I have already talked about performance coaching, and sports coaching is essentially a subset of this. However, I have given it its own section as it is sometimes not seen in this light – a mistake in my view.

Many top sports coaches are NLP trained, and NLP can help a sportsperson prepare for the mental aspect of the game, with visualisations, rituals and anchoring techniques.

Remember, of course, that modern coaching began with Timothy Gallwey's new method of demonstration and repeated actions: the client learns through doing, rather being told what to do. The modern sports coach is well advised to learn NLP questioning techniques, asking 'How would you do x ...?' to encourage self-examination and motivation.

The material on weight loss that I presented in the previous chapter is equally applicable to fitness development (sadly, I see many more people troubled by the former than eager for the latter).

The Circle of Excellence is an ideal pre-performance tool.

At a deeper level, the Meta Model is a powerful way of discovering limiting beliefs, which can then be challenged and changed. And deeper still, processes like the Hero's Journey and

Rescripting can bring about change at the Identity level, which is probably essential in creating the right mindset in which to do sports in a way that is both highly competitive and enjoyable.

Modern sports is essentially an 'inner game': the difference between the best and the rest is largely mental, and NLP is the best way I know to hone the mind.

There is one specific sports technique that I would like to go into in more detail, as it has uses beyond pure sports work.

Modelling and inner rehearsal

By using NLP, sportspeople can practise their game in their own mind.

From a neurological perspective, the mind cannot tell the difference between reality, fantasy and dreams: the same brain-wiring and psychological responses occur regardless of whether the game is real or imagined. Therefore, mental rehearsal reinforces the hardwiring of the brain to improve performance. The dopamine system can actually learn unconscious skills by this type of practice, by imagining different scenarios.

Part of NLP is modelled on the famous hypnotherapist Milton Erickson, who as a teenager was confined to an iron lung, his body completely paralysed. Milton 'copied' the movements of his baby sister: as she learnt to walk, he imagined himself firing the relevant muscle groups in his legs, as if he were learning to walk, too. Although the doctors diagnosed he would never walk again, he proved them wrong, and ended up taking a 1,200-mile canoe trip on his own, returning able to walk with the help of a stick.

The principle of activating muscle groups with your mind (called micro-muscle modelling) enables a combination of the senses to take place in passive environments. Imagine making a tennis serve while sitting on a crowded bus … The player imagines a movie image of themselves doing it, and at the same time activates the relevant muscle groups *without actually making significant movements* (passengers on the bus are not being knocked over!). Once this combination of visual and kinaesthetic is mastered, the player can rehearse in almost any imaginable situation.

People who find it hard to imagine pictures can have a sense of their body moving rather than a picture. This is based on proprioception, an unconscious, inner sense of our physical location, which is controlled in our inner ear.

Children naturally copy movements without thinking; they just do it and learn complex skills such as walking. This form of direct physical learning, without conscious thinking, is not taught formally, often due to the intellectual bias in our education system. But it can be a good way to acquire new habits or to acquire gestures that we use as positive anchors. Even if we are not sporty, we can learn from sport and its practitioners.

Coaching with family and friends

> Every parent should remember that one day their child will follow their example instead of their advice.
>
> Anonymous

I very much believe that the skills of a coach are useful in relationships with families and friends. Being able to listen to children at key points in their development, without judging them but simply being with them and allowing the answer to emerge, could make all of the difference. And the influencing approach of coaching is hugely valuable when children get to the age at which any attempt to force them in a direction becomes counterproductive.

NLP coaching skills and attitudes such as empathic listening, not being judgemental and asking useful questions are all part of being a good life partner or even just a good friend. And is Rogers' unconditional positive regard not a part of love itself?

A few words of warning, however ...

You can't 'be a coach' for people close to you. The value that the coach adds is that he or she brings many good things associated with successful relationships but is actually a disconnected outsider. You and the people close to you, on the other hand, are connected. In many cases, you will be part of the problem (even the case for the nicest of people). The idea, for example, that you can play the role of a completely detached coach with your kids one minute and tell them off the next is over-optimistic. Children need parents who can from time to time discipline them and set boundaries: playing the coach too much weakens this essential role and can lead to a form of laissez-faire parenting that leaves children confused.

What you can do is bring coaching skills to bear from time to time. If a close family member wants a 'tender ear', listening the way a coach does is an ideal way to show your love and care. But remember this is a role you slip into, not the totality of your relationship with that person.

Simple NLP processes, such as the Well-Formed Outcome, can be done with family members. The Meta Model can be useful – in very small doses: having our every statement picked apart for Meta Model violations is not what most of us want after a long day at the office or on a family holiday.

But a strong word of warning goes with some of the material later in this book. Don't try these at home! Parts Integration, Permission and Rescripting share aspects with deep psychotherapy, and these should not be used with your family in any circumstances. These processes harness powerful archetypal energies that can be very healing when conducted by a trusted, experienced outsider. If the processes are conducted by a close family member who is possibly part of the problem, setting these energies loose can be harmful.

CONCLUSION

Coaching and NLP create a mindset of looking at any source for the best ways of handling life, and of harnessing those findings wherever they fit best. Even if sport is not your thing, the internal processes that successful sportspeople use can be hugely helpful when preparing for a challenging meeting. If business is not your thing, learning from great negotiators can help you in a therapeutic setting, using charm and creativity to help a client find a way to overcome obstacles. Taking the best and using it in a different context is a profound gift.

So take this further. Trust yourself to develop your own approaches; use your training and these models to become creative and imaginative in your own unique way.

"Taking the best and using it in a different context is a profound gift."

But what is the next step? There is a big difference between knowing and doing: knowing how to juggle three balls is not the same as being able to actually do the juggling (try it and see!). If you can find time to practise this material, on yourself as well as others, then the doing will feed back into the knowing and you can create a virtuous circle, which will enable you to build excellent coaching skills. I have noticed that students initially find the process of learning a new NLP technique difficult, but by the end of the training they are learning very fast – they see a demonstration, take a few notes and begin the process with a clear idea of what they are going to do: hitting the ground running. In NLP we call this meta-learning, 'learning how to learn', and this is acquired by practice. Clearly, if you can actually attend NLP training, this will speed up your meta-learning considerably.

Then go out and do it! The reason I coach and teach NLP is that I genuinely want people to live happier and more fulfilled lives.

In my life, I found that the demons that initially drove me to success were becoming counterproductive: as I was getting older I was draining my energy, which would ultimately lead to health problems rather than to the affluent future I had promised myself as a young man. I found that by applying the principles of coaching and NLP I could redesign my life, apply personal leadership and succeed without having to burn the candle at both ends. This is the great gift of NLP: it provides processes and a 'can do' attitude that enable you to design the life you want to lead and actually lead it.

To wake up in the morning smiling and looking forward to the day is the greatest gift of this material. I get great pleasure from passing it on to other people, and I hope you will use it to bring joy into your life and the lives of others as well.

Robbie Steinhouse
London, 2010

APPENDIX A

STUDYING NLP

Although I have attempted to make this book as accessible as possible (try reading some other NLP books!), I genuinely believe that NLP is essentially an experiential subject. An NLP book, however good, is always going to be a bit like a cookery book – the actual cooking is much more fun. However, I hope that the material in this book will provide enough information for you to get familiar with the processes and understand the basic philosophy and mindset of NLP.

If you can attend some NLP training, I strongly suggest you do; and if you do, I suggest that you attend one of the longer courses, typically 130 hours of contact training for NLP practitioners spread out over time. This is the approach I use, as it gives students the time to practise the material and slowly work it into their lives, which is where I believe the real learning takes place. Other people teach NLP more by inspiration, and although they can be very charismatic I think there is no substitute for doing the exercises yourself.

APPENDIX B

SIXTEEN HALLMARKS OF A GREAT NLP COACH

1 **Curiosity** – Every client is unique, and being allowed to enter their personal work is both an honour and fascinating.

2 **Rapport** – The ability to create and sustain it.

3 **Confidence in yourself and in your ability to establish credibility** – Belief in the value and power of your own presence.

4 **Confidence in the client** – The belief that the client has the ability to resolve their own issues and that the coach's essential job is to facilitate this, without undue interference.

5 **Sensory acuity** – The ability to 'read' clients and understand what is going on for them behind what they are saying.

6 **Acceptance** – The ability to enter into the client's map of the world without passing judgement.

7 **Knowledge** – A solid familiarity, theoretical and practical, with all the main techniques, along with an ability to hold and take the best from conflicting psychological models.

8 **Flexibility** – The ability to improvise using your knowledge, in the truest sense of going with the flow of the session and relying on unconscious wisdom to use the right tool at the right time. Being willing to make a mistake is an essential part of this ability.

9 **Care** – Concern for and interest in the client.

10 **Inner strength** – The ability to accept and handle the client's demons. You can look these straight in the eye, however fearsome they may appear, sharing and holding the demons without letting them into yourself.

11 **Robustness** – The ability to ask difficult questions when appropriate.

12 **Patience** – Not pushing the client towards outcomes too quickly, but sowing a seed and giving it space to germinate and grow …

13 … while staying aware that results are what coaching is ultimately about. A quiet focus on results.

14 **The ability to mentor** – Having been in an approximately similar position to that of the client, or having worked with people who have been in that position, and being able to draw on that experience to help.

15 **Empathy and the ability to share it** – 'I sense you …'

16 **Personal integrity** – A belief that who you are is more important than what you do.

APPENDIX C

A CONTRACTING SCRIPT

Introduction to coaching in general ...

Once I've done this introduction and we've agreed the contract of how we will work together, our 'rules of engagement', coaching is mainly about you talking and me asking you questions. It's about getting clear about the issues you want to work on and goals you want to achieve, then about me asking you questions to direct your attention on the steps you may need to take to achieve those outcomes. Coaching is not something I do to you; it is both of us working as equals in a team, working together to enable you to achieve or resolve whatever you bring to a session. It is a 'designed alliance': you as the client take responsibility and ownership for your own progress and the coach is there to support you in this endeavour.

... and to the Coach to Awakener model in particular

I then ask:

Would you like me to explain to you what I believe to be the differences between coaching, mentoring, therapy, consulting and friendship?

And if they say, 'Yes', I launch into quite a long piece about the above. I reproduce what I say here in full – as with all this material, you should develop your own version of this.

Traditionally, a mentor is usually someone who has 'been there and done that' and will share their experience of going through a similar situation to the one that you currently face. The point of being mentored is to spend some time with someone who is highly experienced in this particular area, so you can be positively influenced by the mentor's attitude. I can do this for you, as I have had some experience in your area [*this obviously depends on the relevant differences between your experience and that of the client*] and I can also bring knowledge of working with other clients in similar situations to you and share with you some of their discoveries – names and significant details withheld, of course. But please note that I will never just switch into 'mentor mode', say sharing a story, without first asking your permission to stop being a traditional coach, who does not act in this way.

Therapy is more about resolving issues from the past that are affecting your performance, relationships or wellbeing in the present. I am also qualified in a form of psychology called NLP (which stands for Neuro-Linguistic Programming), and if an issue of this type arises, I have various processes we can go through. As with mentoring, I will not go down this route without explicitly first seeking your agreement.

Consulting is asking a professional to research your business or organisational processes and present a set of ideas of how these could be improved. Although conducting research of this type is not in the remit of coaching, I am familiar with a number of organisational and psychological models and if I believe one might be useful to you to the issue you face, I will once again ask your permission to explain it. This usually only takes a couple of minutes and most clients find this useful.

Friendship resembles coaching reasonably closely: a good friend will listen to you attentively and ask you questions. The differences are that a friend will want to have 'their say' – while in coaching it is a one-way street. Coaching is all about what you want to talk about. And a friend may have an agenda for you – such as 'be like me', which may not suit you. A coach does not have any agenda; I am just here for you.

I then ask them if they want to see a model that summarises these ideas. If they do, I introduce Coach to Awakener. I draw the basic diagram on a pad:

Mission	Awakener
Identity	Sponsor
Beliefs and values	Mentor
Capabilities	Teacher/consultant
Behaviour	Traditional performance coach
Environment	Guide

Then I say:

Let me explain it from the bottom up:

At the level of Environment, I can act as your guide, pointing out books, websites or courses, and making introductions for you. Any introductions I make, I will not personally benefit from as it is important that you understand I have no hidden agendas for you; I will not do any business with you as a client.

At the level of Behaviour, I can act as your performance coach, helping you rehearse for any important forthcoming event so you will perform at your best.

At the level of Capabilities, I can act as your teacher, providing you with information or models that you might find useful. This is similar to the consultant role I mentioned earlier.

At the level of Beliefs and Values, I can act as your mentor, sharing with you what I know about the path you are following and sharing with you helpful attitudes. Coaching may also reveal some conflicting beliefs or values you hold and, if you agree, I have tools to help you overcome them.

At the level of Identity, I can act as your sponsor. Often in life, everyone has some kind of agenda for us: our work colleagues, family and friends even partners. I want you to know that I don't hold any agenda for you and I am here just for you, to support you through these interesting times you face. [*Look the client in the eye during this section and say this with a sense of compassion and integrity.*]

At the level of Mission, I can act as an awakener. I often work with leaders and entrepreneurs who want to clarify a mission for themselves and for the organisation they lead. But for anybody, coaching is an ideal opportunity to help them identify what their calling in life is. This can be very powerful material if you are interested in pursuing this further.

The key point is I can act as your coach at all of these levels. If during the coaching, I sense it might be worth exploring one of these areas with you, I will never do so without asking your permission first. Do you have any questions so far?

Confidentiality

Look the client in the eyes and say sincerely, with a slightly severe tone:

I want you to know that whatever you say to me during the coaching session will be fully confidential. I will not tell anyone about what you have said, no one at all. As a qualified coach, if it came to your attention that I had breached confidentiality there is a complaints procedure under the ICF and you could get me struck off. I would also ask that if I have a personal story I want to disclose to you, would you likewise be willing to keep confidentiality? [Look for a nod of acknowledgement from the client.] Lastly, confidentially extends to whether you want anyone to know you are having coaching: for example, if I met you by chance in the street, would you want me to come and speak to you, or would you object if I told people I was coaching you?

Safety

I want to let you know that coaching is a safe process. I am an experienced coach and I know what to do. It is like a safe container, where the space inside belongs to you, so you can explore whatever you wish to explore. The outside of the container belongs to the coach, so I can remind you of what you wanted to work on and keep you focused on that space if you choose to continue to do so.

Terms, conditions and money

Just a reminder: the charge is £x per session, and we have agreed to a set of y sessions. If you need to cancel a session, I need at least 24 hours' notice and preferably more. If it's less than 24 hours, I usually have to make a full charge – sorry about that, but I'm very busy.

Style

How do you like to be treated?

Challenge and the 'wrong question'

Is it OK if I challenge you? Is it OK if I ask you what I call the 'wrong question'? What I mean by that is that sometimes when I ask you a question, it may be that you sense it is taking you in the wrong direction. When that happens, just say to me: 'That was a wrong question.' As a coach, sometimes I have a certain anxiety that every question I ask you must be brilliant. With permission to make a mistake, I can say, 'This might be a wrong question, but …' and if you feel it is wrong, you just tell me and don't have to answer it.

Accountability

As your coach, I offer you optional accountability. What I mean by that is that most of my clients are usually not held accountable or micro-managed. What I have found with some inexperienced coaches is their already overcommitted clients walk away from a session with a further 20 items to add to their task list, and yet they came to coaching to reduce stress! Therefore, in coaching, accountability is also in your control; if you want me to hold you accountable for something, tell me at the end of the session and I will hold you to it in a pre-agreed way.

Summaries and note-taking

How do you learn? And how will you be able to feed forward any discoveries you make within the session? Usually clients either like to ask me to stop for a minute while they take notes, or like to have some time at the end of the session to summarise and carry forward any actions, make notes, etc. This is better than the coach taking notes for you, as I would record what seemed important to me, rather than what was important to you. It also avoids any confidentiality issues arising from notes I made being sent to the wrong place.

Loss of momentum

I have found that sometimes a session can be a bit 'ho hum', as if you are treading water, and you may think that coaching is not worth continuing after an experience like that. But I have found that following a session of that sort, the next session is usually very powerful. What I would like to agree with you is that you will complete the agreed package of six sessions so you can properly go through a coaching process and evaluate the entire experience rather than each session individually. Also, I believe in agreeing an end to the coaching from the outset, so you know this is not open-ended. During the final session, we can reflect on how the coaching went and, if it is appropriate, we can agree to continue with another package. Usually I recommend that clients take a little break before continuing. That's one of the good things about coaching: it does come to an end!

APPENDIX D

THE COACHING WHEEL

The wheel usually has eight segments, though you can have a different number if you think that suits the client better.

Each segment represents a significant area of the client's life. An example 'split' is:

- Career
- Money
- Health
- Friends and family
- Partner
- Personal growth
- Fun
- Physical environment.

Suggest this to the client: they might want to tinker with it, and this is fine.

The client then grades their life as it is right now for each segment. 10 is the top score; 1 is a low score. The grading should be realistic: for health '10' is not an Olympic gold medallist but what the client would consider would be super fit for him- or herself.

The exercise should be done quite quickly: a minute or two is enough. The client's first gradings are usually more accurate, and always more telling, than those overridden by conscious rumination.

Here's a wheel filled in:

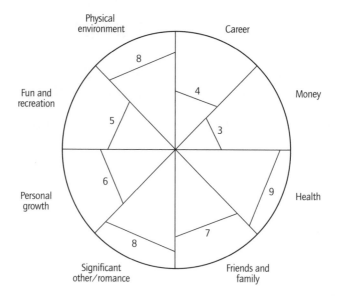

APPENDIX E

SUBMODALITY CHANGES

The techniques in Chapter 10 involve changing the submodalities of internal images, sounds and feelings. Clients can change the way they experience these in an almost infinite number of ways. The list below is a compilation of the ways I have found most useful over the years, but it is not exhaustive. Once clients have got the point that they can tinker with their own internal representations, you can ask them how they would like to change these things, and they will often come up with very creative ways.

Visual

- Nearer/further away
- Change location – up/down/left/right
- Brighter/darker
- Contrast
- Changing colours
- Hue
- Cartoon?
- Photograph
- Movie/still
- Black and white/colour
- Oil painting/watercolour
- Misty or foggy
- Different-colour lights
- Strobe light

- Torch light/spot light
- Through different lenses
- Through a plane-glass window
- With a wood/metal (etc.) frame
- With some other boundary
- Add clothes/make-up/costume/mask.

Auditory

- Location of the source of the sound – up/down/forward/behind/left/right
- Volume – louder/quieter
- Bass – higher/lower
- Treble – higher/lower
- Squeaky
- Rhythm – faster/slower/staccato
- Crescendo/diminuendo – make it gradually louder or gradually quieter
- Faster/slower
- Pitch.

Auditory digital – internal dialogue or recalled voices

Often the changes a coach suggests to internal dialogue are to make it more humorous, in order to reduce the intensity of the memory. Some typical examples are having characters in the memory speak like Marilyn Monroe, Mickey Mouse or Elvis. Say something like 'Change the voice to a sultry sexy voice, like Marilyn Monroe.'

Or have the characters sing – opera can be fun, or rock, or a ballad (and so on …).

Kinaesthetic

■ Location – where in their body does the client have the feeling?

■ Shape – round, square, oval, egg, oblong, tube, two-dimensional, three-dimensional? Like a plate, bowl, ball, spoon (etc.)?

■ Texture – smooth, rough, spiky, sharp, blunt, sticky? Like sandpaper, bubble wrap, glass (etc.)?

■ Hard/soft – flexible, elastic

■ Moving/still – vibrating, circulating, flowing, pulsing

■ Made of …? metal, wood, plastic, paper, leather, fabric, water, syrup, rubber (etc.)?

■ In layers

■ Hot/cold/warm/tepid.

Reading list

Richard Bandler and John Grinder, *Frogs into Princes*

Richard Bandler and John Grinder, *The Structure of Magic*, volumes I and II

Steve Bavister and Amanda Vickers, *Teach Yourself NLP*

Don Beck and Chris Cowan, *Spiral Dynamics*

Eric Berne, *What Do You Say After You Say Hello?*

Shelle Rose Charvet, *Words that Change Minds*

Deepak Chopra, *Quantum Healing*

Stephen Covey, *The 7 Habits of Highly Effective People*

Erik de Haan, *Relational Coaching*

Robert Dilts, *Changing Belief Systems With NLP*

Robert Dilts, *Coach to Awakener*

Robert Dilts, *Modelling With NLP*

Robert Dilts, *Strategies of Genius*, volumes 1, 2 and 3

Milton Erickson (ed. Sidney Rosen), *My Voice Will Go With You*

W. Timothy Gallwey, *The Inner Game of Tennis*

Stephen Gilligan, *The Courage to Love*

Bruce Peltier, *The Psychology of Executive Coaching*

Robbie Steinhouse, *Brilliant Decision Making*

Robbie Steinhouse, *Think Like an Entrepreneur*

Eckhart Tolle, *The Power of Now*

John Whitmore, *Coaching for Performance*

Laura Whitworth *et al.*, *Coactive Coaching*

Ken Wilber, *A Brief History of Everything*

Ken Wilber, *Grace and Grit*

The material on the relative merits of different coaching systems, mentioned on page 6, comes from Bruce E. Wampold's book *The Great Psychotherapy Debate*. It is cited in Erik de Haan's book listed above.

NLP School

the art of change

Dear Reader,

At the NLP School, I present inexpensive and regular public courses, from one-day training events through to full certified NLP Practitioner and Master Practitioner qualifications.

NLP training is an ideal way for people to raise their game in life skills as well as entering on a profound personal development journey. The longer courses are broken down into four or five monthly modules. This gives people the opportunity to practise and absorb the material in their day-to-day life. Over this time, a supportive and friendly culture develops which can be as beneficial as the training itself: delegates become part of a group of people from all walks of life, sharing the desire to make key decisions for positive change. Often close and lasting friendships are formed.

The courses are a rich, effective and enjoyable learning experience. You'll come away with insights and tools you can apply both at work and in the rest of your life – from negotiation, entrepreneurship and leadership, through to self-awareness, cognitive skills, improved relationships, health and inner peace.

All of the ideas in this book are taught on our NLP training programmes.

I hope to meet you on one of my courses.

Warm regards

Robbie Steinhouse

To join an NLP training course or arrange in-house training, visit www.nlpschool.com, email info@nlpschool.com or call us on +44 (0) 207 428 7915.

Index

Note: **Emboldened references** are to **chapters** or word **definitions**